Mastering Python: From Basics to Expert-Level Programming

Learn Python Step-by-Step with Practical Projects

Amelia Hartman

Table of Contents

INTRODUCTION

One of the world's most popular and adaptable programming languages, Python powers everything from automation and artificial intelligence to web apps and data analysis. Both novices and experts will find it a great option because of its ease of use, readability, and extensive library environment. "Mastering Python: From Basics to Expert-Level Programming: Learn Python Step-by-Step with Practical Projects" is your all-inclusive guide to maximizing Python's potential, regardless of your experience level.

This book aims to walk you through all of Python's fundamental ideas, from basic syntax and data structures to more complex programming strategies like concurrency, object-oriented design, and API integrations. Learn the "why" as well as the "how" of Python's most potent features, which will empower you to take on real-world problems with ease.

This book is unique since it emphasizes hands-on learning. Every chapter has practical projects, like making a web scraper, an API-based weather app, and a budget tracker. These assignments are designed to help you see how your skills are directly applied and to reinforce your understanding.

By the time you finish reading this book, you will know how to use Python to tackle challenging issues, build reliable applications, and prosper in a quickly changing tech environment. Let's get you started on the path to Python proficiency!

CHAPTER I

Python Basics

Setting Up the Environment

An essential initial step that establishes the groundwork for your success in learning and using this flexible language is setting up the environment for Python programming mastery. An environment that is set up correctly guarantees seamless development, boosts output, and reduces possible obstacles. Installing necessary software, choosing the appropriate tools, and setting up a neat workspace that supports learning and project development are all part of the process.

Selecting the appropriate operating system for your programming requirements is the initial choice. Because Python is cross-platform, it functions flawlessly on Linux, macOS, and Windows. The particular operating system, however, may have an effect on the tools you select and your process. Developers frequently like Linux and macOS because of its integrated support for Python and command-line tools. To have comparable functionality, Windows users might need to install other software, like Git Bash or Windows Subsystem for Linux (WSL). The objective is to guarantee that Python is installed and available via the terminal or command line, regardless of the platform.

Installing Python itself comes next. Python can be installed via a package manager such as `apt` on Linux or `brew` on macOS, or it can be downloaded from the official website. Unless a particular project or module calls for an older version, it is usually advised to use the most recent stable version of Python. Python must be added to the system PATH during installation. With this setup,

Python commands can be run from any directory without specifically referencing the installation path. Python is correctly set up and ready for use when the installation is verified with a fast command like `python --version` or `python3 --version`.

After installing Python, it is crucial to choose an integrated development environment (IDE) or a text editor designed specifically for Python programming. The coding process is streamlined by features like syntax highlighting, debugging tools, and code suggestions found in IDEs like PyCharm, VS Code, and Jupyter Notebook. Specifically designed for Python, PyCharm offers powerful tools for managing dependencies and virtual environments. Python-specific modifications can improve Visual Studio Code, which is renowned for its versatility. Jupyter Notebook provides an interactive environment that is perfect for running and visualizing code snippets in real time for students and data scientists. Every tool offers benefits, and in the end, the decision is based on your individual requirements and tastes.

Another essential element of configuring a Python programming environment is virtual environments. In addition to avoiding dependency conflicts and guaranteeing compatibility across different libraries and packages, they let you establish separate workspaces for distinct projects. Tools such as `venv`, `virtualenv`, or `conda` can be used to manage virtual environments. Setting up a virtual environment is easy and only requires a few basic commands to activate and populate the workspace. Any libraries installed in this environment are separated from the global Python installation once they are enabled, which lowers the possibility of version conflicts and keeps projects manageable and portable.

Another essential component of learning Python programming is package management. Thousands of libraries and modules that increase Python's capabilities can be found in the Python Package Index (PyPI). You can effectively install, update, and manage these packages with the use of tools like `pip` and `conda.` For instance, installing NumPy with the straightforward `pip install numpy` command gives you immediate access to its robust capabilities if your project calls for numerical computations. Gaining proficiency with package managers guarantees that you can integrate necessary tools, swiftly adjust to new projects, and keep up with the most recent developments in Python development.

Anyone who is serious about learning Python must first configure version control systems like Git. Version control makes it easy to manage several iterations of your code, interact with others, and keep track of changes. You may build repositories, share your work, and participate in open-source projects by installing Git on your computer and connecting it to a GitHub or GitLab account. Knowing how to use commands like `git add,` `git commit,` and `git push` guarantees that your workflow will remain neat and orderly. Beyond working on individual projects, becoming proficient with Git equips you to work in collaborative settings where code management and collaboration depend heavily on version control.

Configuring linters and formatters to guarantee clear and legible code is another part of environment setup. Code is automatically checked for mistakes, style rules are enforced, and ideas for improvement are provided using tools such as Flake8, Black, or Pylint. These tools provide real-time feedback while you develop and work flawlessly with the majority of IDEs and editors. Following best practices and maintaining consistent formatting not only makes your code easier to read but also lowers the possibility of errors and defects.

When setting up your infrastructure, documentation and project management are equally crucial. Files and scripts stay logically organized when you establish a hierarchical folder hierarchy for your projects. Usability and maintainability are improved by adding explicit comments, a requirements.txt file for dependencies, and a README file to your code. For larger projects, creating thorough documentation with tools like Sphinx or MkDocs can give future developers—or even your future self—important information about the organization and intent of your code.

Another important factor to take into account when setting up your Python environment is testing frameworks. You may create and run automated tests using tools like pytest and unit test to make sure your code operates as intended. Early integration of testing into your workflow encourages positive habits and assists in identifying problems before they become significant ones. You may confidently expand and change your codebase without worrying about adding problems if you write thorough test cases.

While frequently disregarded, networking and community involvement are essential components of learning Python programming. Participating in online communities like Reddit and Stack Overflow, visiting meetups, or joining forums can offer opportunities for collaboration on open-source projects as well as insightful information and troubleshooting advice. In addition to improving your educational experience, interacting with the Python community introduces you to cutting-edge methods of problem-solving, best practices, and new trends.

It makes sense to put up domain-specific tools and libraries for people interested in specialist subjects like data science, web development, or machine learning. Installing JupyterLab, Matplotlib, and pandas, for example, may help data scientists analyze and visualize data more efficiently. Those interested in machine learning can install TensorFlow, PyTorch, or sci-kit-learn while aspiring web developers can investigate frameworks like Flask or Django. By extending Python's capabilities, these tools let you work on complex projects and study a variety of topics.

The environment you create as you advance in your Python programming career, becomes a critical factor in facilitating your development and output. The true advantages come from using this environment as a starting point for learning and exploration, even though the first steps concentrate on installing Python, choosing an IDE, and maintaining virtual environments. Now that you have a reliable setup, you can concentrate on learning the language and discovering all of the applications it offers.

Integrating your Python environment into your everyday routine is essential to getting the most out of it. Effective project organization promotes a professional attitude to programming in addition to avoiding clutter. Make sure everything is properly organized and simple to traverse by creating distinct directories for test cases, data files, and scripts. You may further increase your programming efficiency by using tools like GitHub repositories to communicate with others and back up your work.

Because Python is modular, you can customize your environment to fit the unique requirements of your projects. For instance, you may easily incorporate technologies like Beautiful Soup and Selenium into your setup if you're interested in automation. In a similar vein, system administrators can use Python scripts to automate repetitive operations, while game developers can use modules like Pygame to create interactive games. Python's adaptability across a wide range of domains and application cases guarantees its continued relevance.

Learning how to efficiently diagnose and debug your code is a crucial component of becoming proficient in Python. Debugging tools included with modern IDEs let you examine variable values, step through your code line by line, and locate mistakes. Furthermore, Python's built-in stack traces and error messages offer useful information about runtime problems. Gaining proficiency in debugging not only speeds up problem-solving but also expands your knowledge of Python's internal workings.

Version control becomes even more important as the complexity of your projects increases. Any developer must be able to manage several branches, settle merge disputes, and keep a clean commit history. In team environments, where version control systems like Git promote cooperation and guarantee that everyone is working on the most recent codebase, these abilities are invaluable beyond individual projects.

Another important part of learning Python is connecting with other programmers and participating in the community. Local user groups, discussion boards, and online forums are great places to exchange information, get guidance, and find new opportunities. Because Python is open-source, a large number of developers are willing to contribute to collaborative projects, fostering a culture of learning and cooperation. In addition to improving your abilities, being a part of this community gives you access to a multitude of information and viewpoints.

The capacity of a properly configured Python environment to support ongoing learning is one of its frequently disregarded benefits. New libraries, frameworks, and tools are continually being created as the Python ecosystem develops. Maintaining a current environment guarantees that you are aware of the most recent developments and can apply them to your projects. Successful developers who flourish in a field that is dynamic and fast-paced are known for their ability to adapt.

Additionally, as you become more comfortable with Python, think about making your own or contributing to open-source applications. In addition to showcasing your abilities, sharing your work with the larger community allows others to gain insight from your experiences. It's simple to share your ideas, get comments, and work with people all over the world with platforms like GitHub. This degree of participation encourages a feeling of achievement and supports the notion that programming is a creative and team-based activity in addition to being a technical ability.

It takes more than just installing software and configuring tools to create the ideal atmosphere for learning Python programming. It's about establishing an environment where you can develop as a programmer by learning and trying new things. An environment that has been carefully planned allows you to concentrate on the things that really count: learning Python fundamentals, resolving issues, and creating apps that have an impact. By taking the time and making the effort to lay this foundation, you give yourself the tools and self-assurance you need to succeed in Python and beyond.

To sum up, one of the most important steps in your path to proficiency is setting up your Python programming environment. Every element is vital to your growth as a programmer, from setting up the appropriate tools and libraries to planning your projects and interacting with the community. In addition to increasing your productivity, a properly designed environment gives you the freedom to fully utilize Python. Now that you have everything set up, you can start using the language, take on difficult tasks, and enjoy all of Python's endless potential. Your path starts here, and the abilities you acquire will lead to a plethora of programming and other options.

Input and Output

Python programming's core ideas of input and output make them vital tools for communicating with users, files, and other systems. Programs can accept information, process it, and produce insightful feedback or outcomes thanks to these activities. Effective input and output management is essential for developing dynamic and intuitive apps. Python is a flexible and user-friendly programming language that can be used for both basic scripts and complex systems since it provides a large number of capabilities to manage input and output activities.

Python input operations start with collecting information from users or outside sources. Python comes with built-in techniques for interactively handling user input. By using these techniques, programmers can ask users for certain information, such as text, numbers, or other kinds of input. After being gathered, the input can be analyzed, changed, or saved in variables to meet the needs of the application. Developers can easily handle a variety of data kinds and structures thanks to Python's flexible input methods. To guarantee that the program runs dependably even when confronted with unexpected or erroneous data, working with input necessitates careful consideration of data validation and error handling.

Processing user input frequently entails transforming it into the format of choice or carrying out computations using the supplied information. Python's vast library support makes it possible for developers to deal effectively with textual, binary, or numerical data. For example, string techniques can be used to edit text, while mathematical operations can be carried out directly on numeric data. To deal with more complicated input circumstances, such as obtaining particular information from unstructured material, regular expressions, and parsing techniques are also available. Programmers can develop apps that adjust to different user needs and deliver customized responses or outcomes by being proficient in input processing techniques.

Conversely, output procedures entail presenting data to people or storing it for later use. Python offers straightforward yet effective capabilities for producing output in a variety of formats, including highly prepared documents and plain text. A fundamental skill for Python developers is the ability to print messages, results, or error notices. This allows them to debug their code as it is being developed or to communicate with users in an efficient manner. Beyond simple output, Python enables programmers to format their messages using formatting techniques like string interpolation, producing outputs that are not only readable and visually pleasing but also informative.

Handling file operations is one of Python's main advantages when it comes to output capabilities. Programs can store data that can be retrieved or altered at a later time by using files as a persistent storage medium. Python has a number of functions for working with files, such as the ability to write new data to files, read data from files, and append information to already existing files. Developers can regulate how data is read or altered by opening files in various modes, guaranteeing that their programs meet certain specifications. File handling is a fundamental component of many Python applications since it is necessary for operations like data logging, configuration management, and report generation.

The input and output capabilities of Python extend beyond text-based processes. Developers can work with photos, audio files, and other non-textual media thanks to the language's support for binary data. Applications involving multimedia material, encryption, or low-level data processing benefit greatly from binary input and output. Python developers can broaden the scope of their projects to encompass a variety of use cases and industries by learning how to handle binary data efficiently.

An essential component of Python input and output processes is error management. Programs must be made to gracefully manage failures since user input and other data sources are inherently unpredictable. Strong exception-handling features in Python enable programmers to foresee and handle possible problems like incorrect input, file not found errors, or permission problems. Developers can produce more robust and user-friendly apps by integrating error handling into their code, which prevents unforeseen issues from causing program crashes or data loss.

Python's advanced input and output methods need the use of structured data formats like XML, CSV, and JSON. Python's built-in libraries facilitate the parsing, generation, and manipulation of these formats, which are frequently used for data transmission between systems or applications. For instance, developers can load data from a JSON file, make necessary modifications, and then save the modified data back to the file using Python's JSON module. In a similar vein, developers can effectively handle tabular data by working with CSV files, which makes it perfect for uses like data analysis, reporting, and database import. Python developers may efficiently interact with real-world data and integrate their applications with other systems by mastering these sophisticated approaches.

Python's support for network connectivity considerably improves its handling of input and output. Python's socket programming features allow developers to transmit and receive data over networks, allowing them to build programs that communicate with distant servers, web services, or APIs. To retrieve data from an API, for example, a Python program can issue an HTTP request, parse the response, and show the user the results. Python developers should be proficient in network input and output operations since they are essential to creating web apps, chatbots, and distributed systems.

Working with databases is another important area of Python input and output. To connect to databases and carry out tasks like accessing, inserting, updating, or deleting data, Python offers tools like SQLite, SQLAlchemy, and PyMySQL. Developers may effectively store and retrieve vast amounts of structured data by incorporating database capabilities into their apps. Python is a flexible option for developers working with relational or non-relational databases because of its database libraries, which support a variety of database management systems. Building scalable and data-driven apps requires an understanding of database administration and input/output management.

Python's capability for multiprocessing and multithreading likewise heavily relies on input and output activities. Simultaneous input and output activities are common in programs that need asynchronous or parallel processing. With the help of Python's concurrent programming tools and asyncio module, developers can effectively handle these responsibilities and maintain the responsiveness and performance of their programs. An asynchronous Python program, for instance, can read user input, execute calculations, and output the results to a file all at once, enhancing user experience and overall performance.

Gaining proficiency with Python's input and output requires testing and troubleshooting. Developers need to make sure that their programs consistently generate the intended output and handle a variety of input conditions correctly. Developers can create automated tests that verify their input and output logic using unit testing frameworks like unit test and pytest, identifying flaws early in the development process. Debugging tools, like Python's pdb module, let programmers examine variables and walk through their code to find and fix problems with input and output processes. Python developers may produce dependable and sturdy apps by using a methodical approach to testing and debugging.

With new versions and libraries, Python's input and output capabilities keep improving. For developers who wish to use the newest tools and methods, staying current with these developments is crucial. Recent Python releases, for instance, have added f-strings and other capabilities that make string formatting more efficient and concise, which makes it simpler to produce complex output. In a similar vein, new libraries and frameworks offer more features for managing specific input and output tasks, like interacting with real-time data streams, message queues, and cloud storage. Python developers may make sure their abilities stay competitive and relevant in a constantly shifting market by keeping up with these advancements.

Input and output management becomes even more complicated for real-time applications. Chat systems, streaming services, and Internet of Things solutions are examples of applications that need minimal latency and continuous data flow. With the help of libraries like asyncio and Twisted, Python's asynchronous programming features enable developers to effectively manage real-time input and output activities. This method guarantees that the program maintains responsiveness while handling several data streams at once. Python has thus gained popularity among developers creating real-time systems in industries like entertainment and financial.

The growing popularity of serverless architecture and cloud computing is also greatly aided by Python's input and output capabilities. Data sharing with cloud platforms, APIs, and distributed systems is a common feature of modern applications. Developers can upload files, retrieve data, and interact with cloud-hosted databases by using Python libraries like boto3 and google-cloud-storage, which make input and output operations with cloud services easier. Python programs can now function in a global, scalable, and highly available environment thanks to these integrations.

Input and output activities must take security into account, especially for applications that handle sensitive data. To avoid vulnerabilities like SQL injection, cross-site scripting (XSS), or data leaks, Python writers must follow best practices to make sure that inputs are cleaned and outputs are safely handled. Tools for encrypting and hashing data are provided by libraries like cryptography and hashlib, which give input and output procedures an additional degree of security. Developers may increase user trust and guarantee adherence to industry standards and regulations by putting security first.

Python is a flexible tool for integrating with cutting-edge technologies like edge computing, robotics, and blockchain because of its flexibility in handling input and output. Python's libraries and frameworks are well-suited to handle the unique data formats and real-time processing requirements that are frequently associated with these disciplines. For instance, robotics systems need Python for sensor input and actuator output, while blockchain applications can need Python scripts to read and write data to distributed ledgers. Developers can use Python's advantages to innovate and tackle challenging problems in cutting-edge fields by becoming proficient in input and output operations.

Libraries and frameworks that encapsulate the complexity of input and output processes have also emerged as a result of Python's ecosystem's growth, freeing developers to concentrate on higher-level logic. For instance, frameworks like Django and Flask make it easier to handle HTTP requests and responses, which facilitates the development of online applications. These frameworks handle input and output tasks in the background, freeing up developers to concentrate on creating business logic and user interfaces. The time and effort needed for implementation are further decreased by streamlining input and output processes for web scraping and browser automation with the help of automation tools like Selenium and Scrapy.

When considering the function of input and output in Python programming, it is clear that these actions serve as the foundation for almost all applications. Python's many features allow programmers to design programs that are strong, effective, and easy to use, whether they are reading user input, processing files, or communicating with databases and APIs. Programmers can bridge the gap between abstract computing and practical application by being proficient in input and output operations. This allows them to transform raw data into meaningful experiences and actionable insights.

To sum up, Python programming relies heavily on input and output procedures, which facilitate smooth communication between users, programs, and external systems. From simple text processing to sophisticated database, API, and cloud platform interfaces, Python offers a full suite of tools for handling data transmission. Developers may fully utilize Python and create systems that are not just functional but also scalable, secure, and user-centric by devoting effort to comprehending and mastering these processes. Python's ability to handle input and output in a variety of ways guarantees that it will always be a fundamental component of contemporary programming, enabling programmers to address problems in a wide range of fields and industries.

Control Structures

Control structures in Python are fundamental components of the language that allow for decision-making and the execution of specific blocks of code depending on certain conditions or the flow of a program. Gaining proficiency in Python programming requires knowing how to use these control structures. These control structures, which provide Python programs more flexibility and complexity in their behavior, include conditional statements, loops, and exception handling. They make it feasible to create complex applications by enabling a computer to react to various inputs, carry out repetitive activities, and gracefully manage mistakes.

The `if,` `elif,` and `else` statements are examples of conditional statements, which are the most fundamental of these control structures. These enable the programmer to define various courses of action for the program based on whether a particular condition evaluates to true or false. An `if` statement, for instance, determines whether a condition is true before executing a block of code. Depending on whether other conditions need to be examined, the program may move on to an `elif` (else if) statement or an `else` block if the condition is false. This branching structure, which is utilized in almost all Python applications, from simple algorithms to intricate systems, is crucial for the program to make decisions.

While loops are crucial for handling repetitive operations in Python applications, conditional statements manage basic decision-making. The `for` and `while` loops are the two main kinds of loops in Python. The `for` loop is typically used when iterating over a sequence, like a list or range of numbers, or when the number of iterations is known beforehand. It works well for jobs that need the same block of code to be run a certain number of times. Conversely, the `while` loop keeps running as long as a specified condition is true. This kind of loop is helpful in circumstances when the number of iterations is not preset, and the loop must continue until it is terminated by an outside event or condition.

Python's control structures extend beyond loops and conditionals. One effective technique for handling errors and other extraordinary circumstances that could occur while a program is running is exception handling. Python handles failures by using the `try,` `except,` `else,` and `finally` blocks. The `except` section specifies how to handle the exception in the event that it arises, while the `try` block contains code that may raise an exception. If no exception is raised in the `try` block, the optional `else` block is executed. Whether or not an exception occurs, the `finally` block, which is also optional, is always run after the `try` and `except` blocks. This exception-handling framework is very useful for making sure that a program keeps functioning properly even in the face of unforeseen problems.

In more complex Python applications, including those involving user interaction, managing sizable datasets, or interacting with databases and APIs, control structures are also crucial in determining the execution flow. Control structures are employed in interactive programs to direct user input flow and guarantee that, in response to user choices, the appropriate actions are performed. An `if` statement, for instance, could be used by a program that receives user input to determine whether the input satisfies specific requirements and then takes appropriate action. Loops can also be used to ask the user for input repeatedly until they provide a legitimate response.

Control structures are crucial for iterating over big datasets and carrying out operations on individual data components in the context of data processing. A `for` loop can be used to apply a function to each item as it iterates over a collection of objects or a list of numbers. Similar to this, `while` loops can be used to process data until a specific condition is satisfied, such as processing every item in a dataset or waiting for the application to receive the required data from an API or database.

For the management of complex systems, including real-time data processing, machine learning models, and web applications, control structures are also crucial. In these situations, event-driven programming, parallel processing, and asynchronous jobs may all be managed with Python's control structures. Loops, for example, can be used by an event-driven web application to manage HTTP requests, deliver responses, and continuously check for user input. Control structures aid in model training in machine learning applications by iterating through several data batches, modifying weights, and assessing performance at each stage.

Python's control structures are being improved and given new functionality as it develops further. For instance, Python 3.5 made asynchronous programming possible with the introduction of the `async` and `await` keywords. A program that uses asynchronous programming can run several tasks at once without causing the main thread to stall. Applications that need I/O operations, such as web servers or network connections, will find this very helpful. Python programmers may design extremely responsive apps that can manage several tasks at once by combining control structures with asynchronous programming.

Python has a number of sophisticated capabilities, like list comprehensions, lambda functions, and the `with` statement, in addition to these common control structures. These features allow for more succinct and expressive methods of managing program flow. By iterating over an existing list or other iterable objects and applying a modification, list comprehensions, for instance, enable developers to generate new lists. Compared to utilizing conventional loops, this can produce code that is cleaner and more effective. Control structures can use anonymous functions called lambda functions to carry out operations on the fly without having to define a separate function by making sure that resources like files or network connections are handled correctly and cleared up after usage; the `with` statement streamlines resource management.

One of Python's main advantages is the readability and effectiveness of its control structures. Python's syntax is meant to be simple and easy to understand, which helps programmers communicate their ideas more effectively. Python's control structures, in contrast to those of many other programming languages, define code blocks using indentation, which enhances readability and promotes sound programming techniques. Braces and semicolons, which might cause misunderstandings or mistakes in other languages, are no longer necessary thanks to this functionality. Readability is further improved by Python's usage of natural language constructs like `if,` `else,` `elif,` and `while,` which give the control structures a more natural feel.

Python's control structures are performance-optimized to effectively manage a variety of tasks. Python's interpreted nature makes it slower than languages like C++ or Java, but its control structures are made to execute tasks with little overhead. For example, conditional checks can effectively manage Python's `while` loops and the language's `for` loops are well-suited for iterating over huge datasets. Additionally, even in large-scale systems, Python's exception-handling framework enables graceful error management without noticeably affecting performance.

Gaining proficiency in Python programming requires an understanding of control structures, which is crucial for inexperienced programmers. These structures serve as the foundation for more complex ideas like multi-threading, functional programming, and object-oriented programming. Learning control structures gives a programmer a strong basis for taking on increasingly difficult programming problems in addition to improving their ability to design effective and maintainable code. The ability to use control structures effectively will continue to be a crucial skill for developers as Python gains popularity and is utilized in a wider range of domains, including data science, artificial intelligence, and web development.

Python's control structures are more flexible than just loops and conditional expressions. For instance, Python's exception-handling mechanism provides a strong foundation for handling mistakes and exceptions, guaranteeing that programs can manage unforeseen problems without crashing. Developing dependable applications requires this framework, especially ones that communicate with outside resources like databases, networks, or user input. Python developers may control failures and guarantee that specific activities are always carried out, even in the event of errors, by utilizing the try, except, else, and finally blocks. Applications must have this degree of control to function properly, particularly in production settings where dependability and uptime are crucial.

Furthermore, the advent of asynchronous programming in Python, made possible by keywords like await and async, has revolutionized the way programmers create applications that must manage several processes at once. Python programs with asynchronous control structures can execute non-blocking input/output operations, which makes them perfect for systems that need concurrent task management, including web servers and real-time chat apps. The continuous development of control structures and their significance in contemporary programming techniques are illustrated by these recent additions to the Python language.

As you advance in your Python programming career, it's critical to keep in mind that control structures form the foundation of reasoning and decision-making in all programs, not simply essential components of the language. You will be able to develop code that is not just functional but also optimized for efficiency, scalability, and maintainability if you know how to use it properly. Understanding control structures is essential to becoming a skilled Python programmer, regardless of whether you are working on a personal project, supporting an open-source campaign, or creating enterprise-level software.

Python's control structures are powerful because they are straightforward and adaptable. These structures make it possible to write programs that can respond dynamically to changing circumstances, handle failures gently, and adjust to a range of inputs. The control structures in Python offer the framework for almost all programs, from simple apps to intricate systems. The significance of comprehending and being proficient in these structures will only expand as Python develops further, making them a crucial component of any Python developer's arsenal.

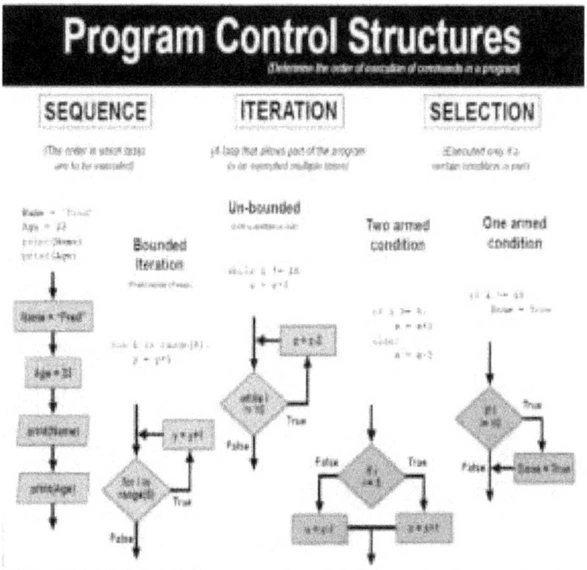

To sum up, Python control structures are essential tools that enable adaptable, legible, and effective program execution. Python offers a wide range of control structures, from the fundamental `if` statements to more complex ideas like asynchronous programming and exception handling, enabling programmers to design complex applications. Programmers can create software that is not only useful but also scalable, safe, and easy to use by becoming proficient with these control structures. Python's focus on readability and simplicity will continue to benefit developers as new control structures and capabilities are added, making it a great option for both inexperienced and seasoned programmers.

CHAPTER II

Core Python Concepts

Functions

Functions in Python are fundamental tools that not only order and simplify code but also bring a sense of clarity and simplicity to the programming process. Python's ability to combine related statements and processes into a function enables code reusability and simpler maintenance. In essence, a function is a block of code designed to carry out a specific task, allowing programmers to break down complex logic into smaller, more manageable chunks. This approach, which emphasizes readability, maintainability, and scalability, becomes increasingly important as the project's complexity grows.

In Python, the `def` keyword, the function name, and a group of parentheses that may include parameters are used to define a function. These arguments allow for dynamic behavior depending on various inputs by serving as placeholders for values that can be provided into the function when it is called. The function can be called by referring to its name and entering the required arguments after it has been defined. Functions can be called more than once, possibly with different arguments, to accomplish the same action because they are made to be reusable. Python applications become shorter and easier to maintain because of this feature, which drastically minimizes the need for code duplication.

Additionally, functions are crucial in assisting developers in creating more debug-friendly code. It is simpler to isolate and find errors when related functionality is divided into distinct functions. It is easy to identify where things are failing when something goes wrong because the issue is frequently linked to a certain function. Furthermore, because functions encapsulate behavior, the program's overall structure is simpler, and the main body of code becomes less crowded. In larger programs, where handling complexity becomes a crucial factor, this arrangement is extremely helpful.

The concept of scope is a crucial component of Python functions that every programmer should understand. When a function is defined, it creates a local scope, meaning that variables defined inside the function can only be accessed within that function. This concept is important as it prevents unintentional changes to variables outside the function's scope. Python's use of local and global variables helps prevent potential conflicts between variables used in different parts of the program, ensuring clean and maintainable code. However, Python also allows variables to be passed into a function, altering its behavior. To avoid mistakes and ensure that functions interact with their surroundings as intended, it's essential to have a solid understanding of how to handle variables and scopes.

Additionally, functions can return values. To return a function's result to the caller in Python, use the `return` statement. Because it enables functions to produce results or carry out calculations that may be utilized or altered in other program sections, this feature is immensely helpful. Functions have a great deal of versatility since they can be used as building blocks for more intricate processes because they can return values. Additionally, it endorses the notion of functions as "black boxes," in which only the inputs and outputs of a function are significant, and the implementation details are concealed.

Python has a variety of more complex function types in addition to basic ones, like anonymous lambda functions that are defined with the `lambda` keyword. Usually, lambda functions are used for brief, disposable functions that don't require names. When a straightforward procedure is required, like in sorting or filtering processes, these routines are extremely helpful. Other complex function types in Python include generator functions, which use the 'yield' keyword to produce a sequence of values, and decorator functions, which modify the behavior of other functions. Although lambda functions can accept several parameters and have a single expression, their functionality is frequently less extensive than that of full functions written using the `def` keyword. Python's emphasis on clarity and simplicity is embodied by lambda functions, which let programmers write useful code with little syntax.

The idea of default parameters in functions is likewise supported by Python. As a result, one or more arguments can be called without explicitly supplying a value. The function employs a preset default value in the event that no value is supplied for such parameters. Because they enable the handling of optional values, default parameters give functions greater flexibility. This is especially helpful when a function may have a large number of parameters, but most use cases only call for a small number of them.

The ability to send an arbitrary number of parameters to a function is another potent feature of Python's function system. The `*args` and `**kwargs` syntaxes are used for this. A function can take a variable number of positional arguments, which are packed into a tuple, with `*args`, and a variable number of keyword arguments, which are kept in a dictionary, with `**kwargs`. Python functions can handle a broad range of input types and configurations because of their flexibility, which makes them extremely adaptable to many situations. When designing functions that are intended to handle varied and variable input, like in complicated data processing or API development, this functionality is quite helpful.

Recursion, which happens when a function calls itself, is a more sophisticated feature that Python offers. One effective method for resolving issues that can be divided into more manageable subproblems of the same kind is recursion. Problems like tree traversal, searching algorithms, and specific mathematical calculations like figuring out the Fibonacci sequence are particularly well-suited for recursive functions. Recursion is a useful tool, but it also necessitates a solid grasp of base case structure in order to prevent the recursion from going on forever. Python is an excellent language for recursive problem-solving because of its recursive features and capacity to manage massive volumes of data.

Another important aspect of Python's function system is higher-order functions. Functions that can return other functions as results or accept them as arguments are known as higher-order functions. Because Python functions are first-class citizens, they can be passed around like other data types and regarded as objects. This enables programmers to write more modular, abstract, and reusable code and opens up a world of possibilities for functional programming. Passing functions to the `map(),` `filter(),` and `reduce()` functions—which are used to handle data collections—is a typical use case for higher-order functions in Python.

Another Python feature that makes use of functions is decorators. Without altering the function's actual code, decorators allow you to change or expand its behavior. In essence, a decorator is a function that accepts an input function and returns a new function with extra capabilities. Python makes considerable use of decorators for purposes like performance monitoring, memoization, access control, and logging. A program's usefulness can be improved without overcrowding its core logic by adding cross-cutting concerns in a clean, modular manner made possible by the ability to attach decorators to functions and methods.

Although functions are useful tools in Python, developers must weigh the trade-offs they entail. Functions, for instance, may result in performance overhead, especially when handling a high volume of function calls. This is due to the fact that every function call requires some degree of context switching and memory management. The advantages of modularity and reusability, however, frequently exceed the performance costs, and Python's functions are built to be extremely efficient. Techniques such as caching, memoization, or rewriting some functions in a lower-level language like C can assist in reducing performance concerns in applications that are performance-critical.

Python functions are crucial for encouraging sound coding techniques in addition to their practical use. Writing brief, targeted functions makes it easier to maintain code that is more tested, modular, and understandable. Developers can write more predictable and debug-friendly code by following the "separation of concerns" paradigm, which assigns a single duty to each function. Because each function is a clearly defined unit of work that can be discussed in a single location, they also make it possible to improve code comments and documentation. In team-based development settings, where several developers could be working on the same codebase, this is extremely beneficial.

Since Python has grown to be one of the most popular programming languages worldwide, developers must be able to build and handle functions efficiently. Knowing how to use functions effectively may significantly enhance the quality of your code, whether you are creating large-scale web apps, data processing pipelines, or small scripts for automation. Functions will undoubtedly continue to be at the core of Python as it develops further, allowing programmers to create clear, effective, and manageable code for many years to come. The more you study Python functions, the more you'll understand how important they are to creating high-caliber software and how they can improve your ability to tackle challenging programming issues. Python's function-based programming style enables you to organize your code in a modular, reusable, and scenario-adaptable manner. Python is the preferred language for developers in practically every industry, from web development to machine learning and artificial intelligence, due to its versatility and strength.

Data Structures

Data structures in Python are not just important, they are a powerful tool for organizing and handling data effectively. Programmers can use them to store, retrieve, and modify data in ways that not only maximize efficiency but also empower them to streamline the development process. Python provides a multitude of tools to address a wide range of computational issues, thanks to its extensive collection of built-in data structures. Gaining proficiency in Python and increasing program efficiency requires an understanding of the many data structures that are available in the language. Python's data structures provide strong tools for managing data in many ways, ranging from basic ones like lists and tuples to more intricate ones like sets, dictionaries, and custom classes.

The fundamental types that are frequently utilized in the majority of programs—lists, tuples, and strings—are not just the foundation of Python's data structures, they are the pillars of adaptability. These data types offer flexible capabilities for storing data sets and are easy to use. Python lists are mutable, ordered sequences that can hold any kind of object. Because of their versatility, they can be used for a wide range of tasks, such as maintaining many data kinds in a single sequence or storing collections of numbers. The ability to index, iterate, and modify lists makes it simple for developers to carry out tasks like sorting data, adding elements, and removing items. Lists have certain drawbacks despite their strength and adaptability, like ineffective additions or removals at the start or middle of the list, which can cause issues for big datasets.

In contrast to lists, tuples are immutable, which means that once they are constructed, their contents cannot be altered. Because of their immutability, tuples are perfect for storing fixed collections of data that shouldn't be changed, such as the members of a fixed set of parameters or the coordinates of a point in 2D space. In terms of access and iteration, tuples are typically faster than lists; nevertheless, they are not modifiable once they are created. Because of this, tuples are an excellent option when data integrity is crucial, and the objects being collected are known in advance.

Another crucial Python data structure for representing character sequences is a string. Similar to tuples, strings are immutable, which means that once they are generated, their contents cannot be changed. Nevertheless, strings provide a wide range of ways to work with their contents, including finding substrings, swapping out segments of the string, and changing characters to other cases. Python is one of the most popular data types for managing textual data because of its highly optimized built-in string handling. For jobs where character manipulation is regularly needed, such as text parsing, data formatting, and user interface design, strings are indispensable.

The set is another crucial Python data structure. An unordered collection of distinct items is called a set, and it is usually employed when an item's existence is more significant than its frequency or order. Tasks like eliminating duplicates from a collection, determining membership, and carrying out set operations like union, intersection, and difference are all frequently accomplished with sets. The main benefit of sets over lists is their speed, especially when it comes to membership testing. Because of Python's highly efficient set operations, developers may carry out tasks like detecting objects that are present in one set but not in another or determining common elements between two sets with unparalleled efficiency.

Another strong Python built-in data structure is dictionaries. A dictionary, often known as a direct, is an unordered set of key-value pairs in which every key corresponds to a distinct value. Dictionaries are extremely flexible and can be used for a variety of purposes, including handling key-value mappings, representing real-world objects such as a person's profile or a product's details, and linking distinct identifiers to data. Because Python dictionaries are implemented as hash tables, lookups, insertions, and deletions can be done incredibly quickly. This makes dictionaries a great option for tasks requiring fast access to data based on unique identifiers, including dealing with associative arrays, managing user profiles, or storing configurations.

Python has the ability to create custom data structures through classes in addition to the built-in data structures. It is possible to define specialized objects that contain both data and behavior by using custom classes. Developers can more easily and systematically represent intricate systems and workflows by building bespoke data structures. To represent a graph, for example, a developer could create a class having methods for traversing the network, joining edges, and adding vertices. Compared to general-purpose data structures, custom data structures frequently offer more effective solutions for specific tasks and offer more flexibility in addressing specialized issues.

The linked list is one of the most significant data structures in computer science and is frequently utilized when frequent insertions and deletions are required or when the size of the data is unknown beforehand. A linked list is a type of linear data structure in which nodes—elements—are connected to one another in a specific order. Every node in the list has a reference to the node after it, as well as a data element. Python custom classes can be used to implement linked lists. Depending on the requirements of the application, each of the several linked list variations—such as singly linked lists, doubly linked lists, and circular linked lists—has pros and cons of its own.

Other basic data structures that are widely utilized in computer science and algorithms are stacks and queues. According to the Last In, First Out (LIFO) principle, a stack is a collection in which the final piece added is the first to be withdrawn. Stacks are frequently used for operations like evaluating expressions, organizing function calls, and undoing actions. Conversely, queues adhere to the First In, First Out (FIFO) principle, which states that the first element added is also the first element withdrawn. Queues are commonly employed in situations such as processing network requests, developing breadth-first search engines, and managing tasks in a job queue. Lists can be used to implement both stacks and queues in Python, but more effective implementations are offered by specialized data structures such as the `deque` class from the `collections` module.

Another crucial Python data structure is heaps, which are frequently employed in algorithms that call for the quick retrieval of the largest or smallest element. Depending on whether it is a max-heap or min-heap, a heap is a binary tree-based data structure that satisfies the heap property, meaning that each node's value is either more than or less than its offspring. In algorithms like heap sort and priority queues, where the primary objective is to swiftly retrieve the element with the highest or lowest priority, heaps are frequently utilized.

One of the most intricate and adaptable data structures, graphs are used to depict the interactions between items in a number of domains, such as social networks, computer networking, and route planning. A collection of vertices, or nodes, joined by edges makes up a graph. Python has a number of graph representation options, including lists of lists and dictionaries. Depending on whether the edges in a graph have a direction, the graph can be categorized as directed or undirected. Additionally, graphs can be weighted, which assigns a value to each edge. To determine the shortest path, identify cycles, or explore every reachable node in a graph, graph algorithms like Dijkstra's algorithm, depth-first search, and breadth-first search are frequently employed.

Another crucial data structure for hierarchical data representation is a tree. A tree, which consists of a root node and subtrees of child nodes, is a specific instance of a graph without cycles. Databases, file systems, and network routing algorithms all frequently use trees. The binary search tree (BST), one of the most popular tree types, maintains a sorted structure that enables quick searching, insertion, and deletion operations. Other tree types include heap trees, B-trees, and AVL trees; each has unique characteristics that make it appropriate for a particular use case.

Understanding the time complexity of data structures in relation to standard operations like insertion, deletion, and searching is crucial when working with them. The term "time complexity" describes how long an algorithm takes to execute as the size of the input increases. For instance, the temporal complexity of finding an element in an unsorted list is O(n), where n is the number of elements, as it necessitates a linear scan of every entry. On the other hand, because of the underlying hash table structure, it is possible to search for an element in a dictionary or a set in constant time, O(1). In order to ensure that programs operate well even with big datasets, developers can make well-informed judgments regarding which data structures to utilize in various scenarios by having a thorough understanding of time complexity.

Any programmer's toolkit must include data structures, and Python's extensive collection of pre-built structures and custom-structure creation capabilities allow developers to tackle a wide range of issues. Writing scalable and effective algorithms requires careful consideration of data structure selection because it can significantly impact algorithm performance. Learning Python data structures enables programmers to create functional and performance-optimized programs that are more suited for large-scale systems and real-world applications. In order to write clear, effective, and maintainable code, Python programmers must master the time complexity and trade-offs of various data structures, as well as when and how to utilize them. Python developers are better prepared to handle challenging computational issues by learning about data structures, which gives them a greater understanding of how data is arranged, accessed, and altered.

File Handling

Working with files, whether to read data from them, write data to them, or change their contents, is referred to as file handling in Python programming. Given that the majority of programs require some kind of file input or output, it is an essential ability for developers. Python enables developers to work with files in a simple way because of its robust and user-friendly file-handling features. In addition to more complex tasks like searching for specific locations inside a file, adding to files, and managing various file formats, file handling includes a variety of basic actions, including opening files, reading data, writing data, and closing files. Python provides versatile ways to handle data storage and retrieval, whether working with text, binary, or CSV files.

Opening a file is the initial step in file handling. The built-in `open()` function in Python is used to open files, giving programmers the ability to choose the mode in which they wish to work with the file. These modes are 'rb' or 'wb' for reading or writing binary files, 'r' for reading, 'w' for writing, and 'a' for adding. A file object that can be utilized to carry out file operations is returned by the `open()` function. Python reports a `FileNotFoundError` if the file does not exist while attempting to open it in 'r' (read) mode. This means that developers must handle such situations gracefully, possibly by verifying that the file exists before attempting to open it.

Developers can work on a file in a number of ways after it has been opened. Reading from a file, which can be accomplished with methods like `read(),` `readline(),` or `readlines(),` is the most often performed activity. The `readline()` method reads a line at a time, which is helpful for processing huge files without using a lot of memory, whereas the `read()` method reads the entire file and returns its content as a string. After reading the full file, the `readlines()` method provides a list of lines, each of which corresponds to a line in the file. When the file size is manageable, these techniques are frequently employed; however, for larger files, reading the file line by line or in chunks may be more effective.

Another essential file management operation is writing to a file. The `write()` or `write lines ()` methods are used in Python to write to a file. While the `write lines ()` method publishes a list of strings to the file, the `write()` method enables developers to write a single string to the file. The contents of the file will be rewritten if it is opened in 'w' (write) mode. When working with files, this is a crucial factor to take into account because unintentional overwriting might result in data loss. Opening the file in 'a' (append) mode will add new data to the end of the file without changing the material that is already there. This is very helpful for logging or for adding new data gradually.

Python offers functions for working with file pointers, which provide the current location within a file, in addition to reading and writing. While the `tell()` function returns the file pointer's current position, the `seek()` method enables developers to shift the file pointer to a specified byte offset. When working with huge files or binary data, these techniques are very helpful since they allow you to navigate to specific areas of the file, which can save time and increase productivity. For instance, you could use the `seek()` method to place the pointer at the end of the file and begin reading from there if you are dealing with a log file and only need to view the most recent data.

Closing files after operations are finished is another crucial component of file handling. To ensure that any modifications are stored and resources are freed, a file can be closed in Python using the `close()` method. After working on a file, it's critical to close it because leaving it open can result in resource leaks and other undesirable behavior. By using the `with` statement, which manages file opening and shutting automatically, Python offers another method for handling files. Because it guarantees that files are correctly closed even in the event of a file operation error, this method is recommended. By automatically managing the file's lifecycle, the `with` statement makes file handling simpler.

Developers also need to be mindful of any exceptions and problems while working with files. Using the `try,` `except,` and `finally` blocks, Python offers a strong exception-handling framework. For instance, a developer may get a `FileNotFoundError` while trying to open a file if it doesn't exist or a `PermissionError` if there aren't enough rights to access it. Developers can gracefully handle mistakes by detecting exceptions and encapsulating file-handling activities in `try` blocks. This allows them to take corrective action or provide users with instructive notifications. Furthermore, even in the event of a mistake, files can be correctly closed by using the `finally` block.

Another crucial component of file management in Python is working with various file formats. Among the most basic and widely used file formats are text files, including plain text (.txt) files. Standard file handling techniques can be used to open and modify these files, which hold data as a string of characters. Working with CSV (Comma-Separated Values) files, which are frequently used to store tabular data, is another feature that Python offers. Python's `csv` module makes it simple for developers to read and write CSV files by handling headers, parsing rows, and outputting data in a standard manner. Another helpful tool for handling structured data in the JSON (JavaScript Object Notation) format—which is frequently used for data interchange between applications—is the `json` module. Developers can deal with JSON data in a way that is both machine-readable and human-readable thanks to the `json` module, which makes it simple to encode and decode JSON data.

Another file type that developers come upon while working with file handling is binary files. Binary files store data in raw byte format, as opposed to text files, which store data as plain characters. By using binary modes ('rb' for reading and 'wb' for writing), Python enables developers to work with data, including compiled code, pictures, and audio files. Because binary files hold data in non-text format and operations like reading and seeking necessitate an understanding of byte-level manipulation, reading and writing them requires extra care. For example, in order to guarantee proper processing and presentation of picture files, the binary data must be interpreted as a series of bytes.

When it comes to directories and paths, file management is equally important. The `os` and `shut` modules in Python offer a number of file and directory management features. Developers are able to create, delete, and list files and directories using the `os` module. In contrast, the `shuttle` module offers higher-level functions for file operations, including renaming, copying, and transferring files. An object-oriented method of managing file paths and an intuitive interface for interacting with file systems are provided by the `pathlib` module, which was first included in Python 3.4. These modules make operations like handling file path modification, establishing new directories, and determining whether a file exists simpler.

Python provides utilities for optimizing file I/O operations for developers who need to work with large files or who need high-performance file handling. One such optimization method is buffered I/O, which enables data to be read or written in bigger chunks as opposed to byte by byte. To indicate how much data should be read or written at once, use the buffer size argument with the `open()` function. When working with huge datasets, this method is more efficient since it uses fewer read or write operations. Although Python's built-in file-handling features are optimized for the majority of use cases, developers can create their own buffering techniques for specific applications that need more control over speed.

Python programming requires file handling because it offers the capabilities and tools required to communicate with external data sources. Python's file-handling features enable developers to tackle a variety of issues, from reading and writing simple text files to working with binary files and specialized formats like CSV and JSON. Python is a versatile and effective language for file-handling jobs because of its strong file I/O operations, which can be used for processing huge datasets, managing configurations, or logging data. Understanding how files function, the various file modes and formats, and the tools available for executing tasks like seeking, closing, and error handling are all essential to becoming proficient with file handling in Python. Developers may build scalable and reliable programs that can communicate with external data in a multitude of formats by mastering Python's file-handling techniques. Furthermore, developers may make sure that their programs stay effective and simple to maintain by utilizing Python's built-in modules for working with directories, paths, and sophisticated file operations. Python's file-handling features offer the versatility and functionality required for almost any activity, whether working with simple text files or processing enormous binary datasets.

Data security and privacy are also essential components of file processing. Python provides tools and libraries for encrypting and decrypting files to guarantee that data stays secure in light of the growing emphasis on protecting sensitive information. File encryption algorithms can be implemented by developers using libraries like PyCrypto and cryptography, enabling safe file transmission and storage. Furthermore, file sharing over networks is made simpler by Python's support for secure file transfer protocols, like SFTP, through the paramiko package. By integrating these safeguards into file handling procedures, user data is shielded from unwanted access, and privacy laws are followed.

Python's flexibility in managing files also applies to specialized fields. For example, processing complex data contained in file formats such as HDF5, NetCDF, or FITS is frequently necessary for scientific and technical applications. Libraries like h5py, netCDF4, and astropy are part of Python's ecosystem and allow for the efficient handling of these specific formats, giving researchers and engineers the means to evaluate and interpret their data. Similarly, libraries like Pillow, wave, and OpenCV-python enable Python to work with multimedia files, including photos, audio, and video. By enabling programmatic manipulation of multimedia data, these libraries pave the way for applications in fields such as image processing, audio analysis, and video editing.

Python's usefulness in today's programming environment is further increased by combining its file management features with cloud-based storage platforms. Developers can save and retrieve files from distant locations thanks to libraries like boto3 and google-cloud-storage, which facilitate smooth interaction with cloud services like Amazon S3 and Google Cloud Storage. Applications and distributed systems that need to obtain data from several sources or offer worldwide file accessibility will find this very useful. Python developers can create adaptable and scalable applications that capitalize on cloud computing advantages by utilizing these integrations.

Additionally, Python offers strong support for file operations testing and error management. Creating test cases for file handling operations is crucial to making sure that programs operate as intended under various conditions. Developers can test their code without using real files by using the unit test and pytest frameworks in Python, which provide tools for building mock file systems and simulating file operations. This method guarantees that file-related errors are discovered early in the development lifecycle and streamlines the testing procedure. Thorough testing and appropriate error handling contribute to the development of robust programs that can smoothly manage unforeseen circumstances like corrupted data, missing files, or network outages during file transfers.

Lastly, it is impossible to overestimate the significance of following best practices in file handling as programming techniques change. Maintainable and scalable codebases can be achieved by integrating logging methods for file operations, naming files and directories according to conventions, and grouping code related to files into reusable functions. The integrity of file data is preserved across development teams and deployment environments when version control systems, such as Git, are used to monitor changes to files and configurations.

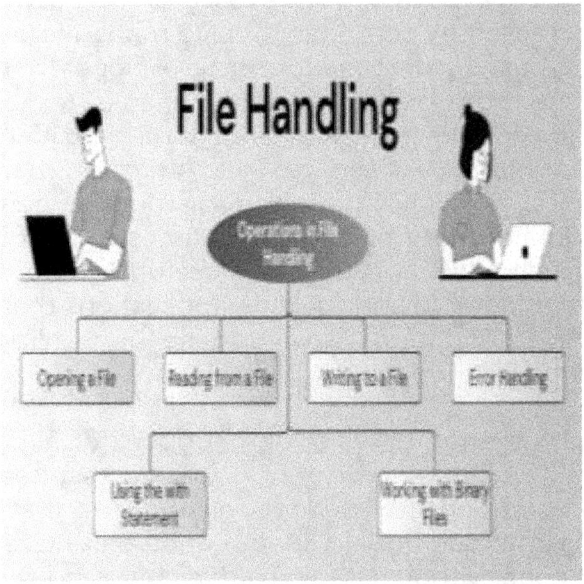

To sum up, knowing how to handle files in Python is crucial for developers to efficiently handle, analyze, and safeguard data. Python is an effective tool for working with files of various sizes and types because of its user- friendly syntax and robust library ecosystem. Python has the flexibility and capability required to handle a variety of file management difficulties, from simple file operations to sophisticated methods for managing big datasets, encrypted files, and cloud integrations. Python's file- handling skills will continue to be a key component of its broad acceptance in fields ranging from automation and scientific research to web development and data science as developers continue to experiment and innovate. Developers may construct apps that are dependable, efficient, and prepared to handle the needs of the contemporary digital landscape by being proficient in file-handling procedures.

CHAPTER III

Intermediate Python Programming

Object-Oriented Programming (OOP)

Python's Object-Oriented Programming (OOP) paradigm is widely considered to be among the most effective strategies for the development and organization of software. Objects, which are instances of classes, provide developers with the ability to model real-world entities and the relationships between them in code. By virtue of its status as a multi-paradigm programming language, Python offers outstanding support for object-oriented programming (OOP) while preserving its simplicity and readability. Encapsulation, inheritance, polymorphism, and abstraction are the four fundamental principles that underpin object-oriented programming (OOP). These principles serve as a guide for developers as they create codebases that are modular, reusable, and maintainable. These characteristics are essential for the construction of sophisticated applications.

The internal state of an object is concealed from the outside world through the use of encapsulation, which is one of the fundamental features of object-oriented programming (OOP). Access to the object is only granted through interfaces that have been clearly defined. Classes and methods are the means by which Python accomplishes this goal. These tools enable developers to specify the characteristics and actions of objects. One way for developers to exercise control over the visibility of properties and methods is through the utilization of access modifiers such as private, protected, and public. In contrast to other programming languages, Python does not rigidly enforce access levels. However, it does provide conventions, such as the prefixing of attribute names with underscores, to indicate the scope of the attributes in question. In addition to improving data security, encapsulation also helps to create code that is cleaner and more structured. This is accomplished by isolating concerns and decreasing the number of dependencies that exist between the various components of a program.

The Python programming language's inheritance feature enables a class to take on the properties and functions of another class, which in turn makes it possible to reuse code and establish hierarchical relationships. Developers are able to design base classes that specify common functionality through the use of inheritance. These base classes can then be enhanced or overridden by classes that are derived from them. This helps to encourage an organized approach to problem-solving while also reducing instances of repetition. Single and multiple inheritance are both supported by Python, providing developers with a great deal of choice when it comes to constructing their class hierarchies. Python, on the other hand, incorporates a method called the Method Resolution Order (MRO) to handle the complexity of conflict resolution that comes along with numerous inheritance styles. Multiple inheritance is made easier to manage thanks to the MRO, which ensures that methods are inherited in a predictable manner by adhering to the C3 linearization technique.

The capacity of distinct objects to respond to the same method call in their own unique ways is referred to as polymorphism, which is another fundamental principle of object-oriented programming (OOP). Method overloading and method overriding are the means by which this is accomplished. Objects in Python are not strictly limited to a particular type, which makes polymorphism extremely useful. Python's dynamic typing makes dynamic typing possible. It is possible for developers to create functions and methods that can be used on objects belonging to other classes, provided that the objects in question already implement the necessary methods. As a result, this results in increased flexibility and code generalization, which enables developers to build programs that are more adaptable and suitable for scaling. The ability to achieve late binding, in which the method that will be invoked is determined at runtime, is another advantage of polymorphism. Late binding makes it possible to create systems that are more dynamic and extensible.

By hiding the technical details of an object and revealing just the characteristics that are absolutely necessary, abstraction is a process that may be described. Through the utilization of abstract classes and interfaces, Python provides support for abstraction. These abstractions can be constructed by utilizing the `abc` module. Abstract classes act as blueprints for other classes, the purpose of which is to define methods that must be implemented by classes that are derived from them. The management and extension of codebases are simplified as a result of this, as it guarantees a consistent interface across all of the different implementations. Not only does abstraction make complex systems easier to understand by concentrating on high-level concepts, but it also improves the readability of code and lowers the likelihood of programming errors occurring during implementation.

Python's Object-Oriented Programming (OOP) features are not restricted to the fundamental principles. Additional advanced techniques, such as class and static methods, properties, and magic methods, are capable of being implemented in this language. Class methods are useful for factory patterns and class-level setups since they operate on the class itself rather than on instances of the class. Static methods, on the other hand, are utility functions that operate within the context of a class. They are not dependent on either the class or the instances the class is associated with. In order to enable the encapsulation of logic within attribute access, properties offer a means via which calculated attributes can be defined. It is possible for developers to define the behavior of objects for built-in operations by utilizing Python's magic methods, which are also referred to as dunder methods. The implementation of the `__add__` method, for example, allows for the customization of the behavior of the `+` operator. Additionally, the `__repr__` and `__str__` methods determine the manner in which objects are represented as strings. Python's Object-Oriented Programming (OOP) model is highly expressive and versatile as a result of these qualities.

The process of creating and developing sophisticated software systems is one of the most intriguing applications of object-oriented programming (OOP) in Python. Object-oriented programming (OOP) makes modularity easier to achieve by partitioning a system into smaller, more independent parts. The fact that each component is encapsulated within a class, which is a representation of the component itself, makes it simpler to comprehend and maintain. Additionally, this modularity makes it possible to conduct better testing and debugging, as individual classes may be tested independently of one another. OOP also encourages the reuse of code through inheritance and polymorphism, which cuts down on the amount of time and effort required for development. In large-scale projects, the hierarchical structure of classes helps to maintain consistency and coherence, which in turn makes the system easier to explore and extend.

One further important advantage of object-oriented programming in Python is that it works well with design patterns. Many design patterns are fundamentally object-oriented, and they are proven solutions to recurrent challenges in software design. Design patterns are also known as design patterns. Singleton, Factory, Observer, and Strategy are examples of patterns that make use of

Object-Oriented Programming (OOP) principles to handle common issues in software development. Python is an appropriate language for implementing these patterns because of its simplicity and versatility. This enables developers to construct systems that are both resilient and scalable. The Factory pattern, for instance, makes use of polymorphism in order to generate objects in a dynamic manner based on specific criteria, whereas the Observer pattern depends on abstraction in order to establish a decoupled relationship between observers and subjects.

In addition, object-oriented programming (OOP) is involved in the frameworks and libraries that are utilized extensively in Python development. For example, web frameworks such as Django and Flask rely heavily on object-oriented programming (OOP) ideas in order to provide an organized approach to the process of constructing web applications. Models in Django are used to represent database tables in the form of classes. These models encapsulate the logic for validating data, querying queries, and manipulating data. In a similar manner, blueprints are utilized in Flask for the purpose of organizing application components into modular parts, which in turn promotes reusability and maintainability. Windows, buttons, and other graphical user interface (GUI) elements are represented as objects with their properties and behaviors in graphical user interface (GUI) frameworks such as PyQt and Tkinter. Object-oriented programming (OOP) is also critical to these frameworks.

For the purpose of managing data pipelines, models, and workflows, object-oriented programming (OOP) in Python is a crucial tool in the field of data science and machine learning. Object-oriented design is the foundation upon which libraries such as Pandas, NumPy, and sci-kit-learn are constructed. These libraries provide classes and methods that facilitate the process of data manipulation and analysis. Machine learning models, for example, are implemented as classes in sci-kit-learn. These classes provide methods for training, prediction, and assessment. This encapsulation of functionality within objects makes it simpler to experiment with a variety of models and configurations while yet preserving a codebase that is clean and well-organized. Additionally, Object-Oriented Programming makes it easier to include bespoke components into pre-existing workflows, which enables data scientists to build solutions to tackle particular issues.

The support for object-oriented programming (OOP) in Python continues to be a fundamental component of the language's versatility and popularity. Because of the language's emphasis on readability and simplicity, object-oriented programming (OOP) ideas are made available to developers with varying degrees of expertise. Additionally, the language's extensive ecosystem of libraries and frameworks heightens the significance of these concepts. A powerful toolbox for turning ideas into code that is functional, efficient, and manageable is provided by object-oriented programming (OOP) in Python. This toolkit can be utilized for the development of web applications, the creation of data-driven solutions, or the design of complex software systems. The full potential of Python may be unlocked by developers who have mastered the ideas and practices of object-oriented programming (OOP). This allows them to create solutions that are not only effective but also adaptive to the always-shifting landscape of technology.

Object-oriented programming in Python has a wide range of practical applications, including but not limited to web development, data research, machine learning, graphical user interfaces, and more. Through its compatibility with design patterns, frameworks, and libraries, it demonstrates the adaptability and usefulness of Object-Oriented Programming principles in the real world. In addition, the extensive ecosystem of tools and resources that Python provides makes it possible for developers to construct complicated systems while keeping an emphasis on the readability and reuse of code.

The demand for object-oriented solutions that are well-structured is expected to continue to increase as technology continues to advance. By utilizing the object-oriented programming (OOP) capabilities of Python, developers are able to efficiently handle these difficulties and create software that can withstand the test of time. Developers are equipped with the abilities necessary to negotiate the complexity of modern programming and make meaningful contributions to the ever-expanding area of technology when they have a strong understanding of object-oriented programming (OOP) in Python. This is true regardless of whether they are working on small projects or large-scale applications.

The conclusion is that Object-Oriented Programming (OOP) in Python is a fundamental paradigm that gives developers the ability to design software that is effective, scalable, and easy to maintain. In order for developers to build systems that are not only robust but also intuitive and modular, they need to have a solid understanding of object-oriented programming (OOP) principles such as encapsulation, inheritance, polymorphism, and abstraction. Python is a good language for learning and using these principles because of its simplicity and versatility. It enables both novice and experienced programmers to construct solutions for a broad variety of domains, making it an ideal language for learning and applying these concepts.

Error and Exception Handling

Error and exception handling is an integral part of Python programming that ensures programs can handle unexpected situations gracefully and maintain robustness during execution. Being a very dynamic and adaptable language, Python offers a wide range of tools and methods for efficiently handling errors and exceptions. These safeguards enable programmers to foresee possible problems, react to them sensibly, and stop unexpected program crashes. Developers can improve a program's maintainability, user experience, and dependability by implementing appropriate error handling.

Python errors usually happen when the program runs into situations it is unable to handle or run. Syntax errors, logical errors, invalid inputs, or outside variables like unavailable resources or unsuccessful network connections can all cause these problems. Runtime problems happen while the program is running, whereas syntax errors are found by the Python interpreter during the compilation stage and need to be corrected before the code can execute. Runtime problems, sometimes known as exceptions, interfere with a program's normal operation and call for specific handling techniques.

Python manages exceptions using a strong exception-handling architecture built on the `try-except` construct. The interpreter stops the current block's execution when an exception is raised and searches for a suitable `except` block to handle the error. The accompanying code runs if a matching `except` block is discovered, enabling the program to recover and carry on. An error notice is shown, and the application ends if there isn't a block of that type. Without sacrificing program stability, this methodical approach to exception management guarantees that possible problems may be foreseen and handled efficiently.

Apart from the fundamental `try-except` construct, Python offers a number of improvements that increase the adaptability and lucidity of handling exceptions. Developers can provide code that will only run if there are no exceptions within the `try` block by using the `else` clause. The program logic is made clearer by this differentiation between typical and unusual flows of execution. Another strong feature that ensures cleanup code is executed whether or not an exception was triggered is the `finally` section. This is very helpful for releasing resources, shutting down files, or carrying out other crucial operations that need to be completed regardless of the state of the program.

Another important tool that helps developers deal with failures methodically is Python's exception hierarchy. The `BaseException` class is the root of the class-based hierarchy that Python uses to organize exceptions. Many common exception classes, including `Exception,` `ArithmeticError,` `IOError,` and `ValueError,` are derived from `BaseException.` Developers can handle these exceptions separately or group them using their parent classes, each of which indicates a distinct kind of mistake. Depending on the needs of the application, this hierarchical structure allows for more granular or broader handling of exceptions, which streamlines error management.

Python's error-handling mechanism is made even more flexible with custom exception classes. To represent application-specific mistakes, developers can create their own exception classes, giving them more control and clarity over how these errors are handled. These new exceptions can be easily integrated with the current error-handling systems by inheriting from Python's built-in exception classes. In big or complex programs, where it is essential to differentiate between various error kinds for debugging and maintenance, custom exceptions are especially useful.

Python error handling extends beyond exceptions that the program raises. Additionally, developers are able to foresee and control problems that come from outside sources, like network interactions, file operations, and user input. Programs frequently need to verify user input, for example, to make sure it satisfies predetermined standards. Developers can gracefully tolerate invalid inputs, ask the user to fix them, and keep the program flowing by utilizing exception handling. In a similar vein, resolving situations like missing files, permission issues, or read/write failures is a common part of file operations. To handle these problems without interfering with the user experience, developers can encapsulate file-related functionality in `try-except` blocks.

In distributed and networked applications, where failures might be caused by outside variables like server outages or connectivity problems, exception handling is also essential. For network communication, Python has libraries like `requests` and `socket,` which frequently produce exceptions in the event of errors. The program can react appropriately by retrying the operation, reporting the error, or alerting the user if these exceptions are handled correctly. This resilience is especially crucial in situations like real-time data processing systems or e-commerce platforms where continuous functioning is essential.

Another crucial component of mistake and exception management that enhances Python's built-in features is logging. Python's `logging` module allows programmers to systematically capture error messages, stack traces, and other diagnostic data. Developers can spot trends, identify problems, and track the application's health over time by keeping thorough logs. By giving context regarding the state and behavior of the program at the moment of an error, logging also helps with debugging. Additionally, structured logging formats like JSON make it easier to integrate with error tracking and monitoring tools, improving the application's overall observability.

Writing understandable and manageable error-handling code is crucial, according to best practices for Python programming. Using specialized exception types instead of generic ones is one such method. Catching general exceptions like `Exception` or `BaseException` might complicate debugging and hide the error's underlying cause. Rather, developers are urged to manage particular exceptions, which offer more insightful details about the source of the problem. Furthermore, since it might result in complicated and inefficient code, it is discouraged to employ exception handling excessively for flow control. Instead, programmers ought to make an effort to build reliable code that employs error handling sparingly and reduces the possibility of exceptions.

Context managers are another recommended practice that makes resource management easier. The `with` statement is used to construct context managers, which make sure that resources like files, sockets, and database connections are acquired and released correctly. Developers can steer clear of typical problems like resource leaks and inconsistent states by encapsulating resource management behind a context manager. This lowers the possibility of errors and enhances code readability, especially in intricate or concurrent systems.

Python software testing and debugging also heavily rely on error handling. Test cases for managing certain exceptions are frequently included in unit tests, which are built using frameworks like `unit test` or `pytest.` Developers can guarantee the program's robustness and dependability by confirming that it operates as intended under a range of error scenarios. Additional assistance for locating and fixing issues is offered by debugging tools, such as integrated development environments (IDEs) or Python's built-in `pdb` module. Developers can expedite the process of identifying and resolving problems in their code by combining these tools with efficient error-handling techniques.

Python's asynchronous programming capability adds more error-handling factors to the mix. It might be difficult to identify and handle mistakes in asynchronous programs since exceptions can arise in concurrently running operations. Mechanisms like `gather` and `wait` are provided by Python's `asyncio` module to manage errors in asynchronous activities. Maintaining the integrity of the application and preventing minor problems that can result from unhandled exceptions in concurrent contexts need proper error handling in asynchronous programming.

Python programming's error and exception management features continue to be essential as software systems get more complicated. Developers can produce programs that are not only functional but also resistant to unforeseen circumstances by grasping these ideas. Python offers a strong basis for creating dependable and maintainable systems because of its extensive error-handling features, best practices, and related tools. Success in Python programming requires knowing and using efficient error-handling mechanisms, whether creating little scripts or complex systems.

The significance of methodical error handling is further highlighted in larger applications. Modules, libraries, and services become more interdependent as codebases expand, increasing the possibility of unanticipated failures. Developers can reduce these risks and produce scalable, stable systems by putting in place a clear error-handling strategy early on. Here, modular design is important because it enables each component to manage faults locally while transferring important problems to higher levels. By ensuring that mistakes are handled at the most suitable level, this tiered method improves the application's usability and clarity.

Strong error-handling procedures also promote team collaboration. Clear exception-handling conventions guarantee consistency across modules when several developers work on the same codebase. These conventions frequently contain instructions on how to use logging frameworks, define custom exceptions, and implement retries for temporary problems. By pointing out places where error handling might be made simpler or better, code reviews serve to further support these procedures. In the end, this cooperative effort produces software that is easier to maintain and more dependable.

Effective error management not only increases code reliability but also enhances user experience. User satisfaction and confidence are increased by applications that fail gracefully, offer insightful error messages, and recommend remedial activities. When a web application detects a server error, for example, it may show a user-friendly message outlining the problem and suggesting other courses of action, such as calling support or retrying the request. In addition to avoiding annoyance, these actions show a dedication to professionalism and excellence.

Error handling plays a part in both the deployment and operation phases, in addition to the development process. Error logs and exception reports are used by monitoring and alerting systems in production situations to identify problems instantly. Teams may gather, examine, and display error data with the help of tools like Sentry, Logstash, or Prometheus, which offer important insights into how applications behave. Decisions about feature development, resource allocation, and performance optimization might be influenced by these findings. Organizations can guarantee the long-term viability of their applications by seeing error management as a continuous procedure as opposed to a one-time event.

Another crucial component of error handling in Python programming is security considerations. Negligently handled errors can give bad actors access to private data, like database credentials or stack traces. Developers should limit the amount of data that is accessible, sanitize error messages, and set up secure logging procedures to avoid such vulnerabilities. By taking these safeguards, the application is not only shielded from any threats but also complies with industry standards and data protection laws.

Python error handling also touches on software engineering concepts like fail-fast design and defensive programming. By focusing on foreseeing and resolving possible problems before they arise, defensive programming lowers the possibility of mistakes occurring during runtime. This strategy is supported by methods like input validation, boundary checks, and type annotations, which help programmers write more reliable code. On the other hand, fail-fast design promotes early error detection, enabling programs to stop right away when serious problems arise. By making debugging easier and avoiding downstream faults, this technique eventually raises the software's overall quality.

It is impossible to overestimate the educational benefit of learning Python's error and exception handling. For novices, grasping these ideas lays a strong basis for addressing more complex subjects like testing, debugging, and performance optimization. For seasoned coders, improving their error-handling abilities improves their capacity to train others and create intricate systems. Furthermore, these abilities are useful in any developer's toolbox because they may be applied to many programming languages.

To sum up, the ability to handle errors and exceptions in Python programming is essential for creating dependable, approachable, and safe applications. Developers can build systems that withstand unforeseen circumstances by utilizing Python's extensive error-handling capabilities, following best practices, and including auxiliary tools.

Beyond its technical advantages, efficient error management promotes improved user experiences, more efficient teamwork, and the long-term viability of applications. Learning error handling will continue to be crucial for developers who want to be the best at what they do because Python is still used in many different fields, including data science, web development, and artificial intelligence.

Modules and Packages

Python modules and packages are essential building blocks that let programmers efficiently arrange, structure, and reuse code. These techniques benefit code readability, maintainability, and team cooperation by breaking up large codebases into smaller, more manageable chunks. In essence, a module is a single Python file that has a collection of variables, classes, and functions intended to carry out a particular activity or a collection of related tasks. In contrast, a package is a group of modules arranged in directories, enabling a hierarchical structure suitable for more complicated and expansive applications. These tools enable developers to create clear and effective programs and are essential to Python's design philosophy of simplicity and modularity.

One important feature that makes using modules and packages easier in Python is the import system. Developers can avoid starting from scratch by importing modules, which provide them access to pre-written code that they can use in their systems. Because of this system's great versatility, entire modules, certain functions, or classes can be imported. When working on large-scale projects, the ability to design and import custom modules is especially helpful because it allows teams to assign tasks to different team members and concentrate on different areas of the program. Additionally, Python's vast standard library includes a multitude of pre-built modules for tasks ranging from data analysis and machine learning to file management and web development, greatly speeding up development time.

Using modules and packages requires an understanding of namespaces. Because each Python module runs in its own namespace, naming conflicts are avoided. For instance, since the functions are accessed using the names of the corresponding modules, two distinct modules can define a function with the same name without encountering any problems. In collaborative settings, when several engineers contribute code to the same project, this capability is extremely crucial. Namespaces keep the code structured and conflict-free by enclosing functionality into discrete modules.

By giving modules a means to be organized into directories, packages expand on the idea of modules. The existence of a `__init__.py` file, which may be empty or contain the package's initialization code, identifies a package. Developers can arrange relevant modules together using the packages' hierarchical structure, which logically reflects the project's structure. In large applications, where the codebase may comprise hundreds of modules, this is especially beneficial. Developers can more easily explore the code and find specific functionality by grouping modules into packages.

The Python Package Index (PyPI) provides access to third-party packages, which is another potent feature of Python programming. The global Python community has created thousands of packages for PyPI that span a vast array of features. The process of acquiring, installing, and managing these packages is made easier by tools like pip Python's package installer. Developers can save time and effort by utilizing pre-existing solutions for common issues thanks to this ecosystem of third-party packages. For example, Flask and Django are utilized for web development, TensorFlow and PyTorch are used for machine learning, and NumPy and Pandas are popular libraries for data analysis. These packages' accessibility has greatly increased Python's appeal and adaptability.

Python development frequently involves the creation of unique modules and packages. Developers can encapsulate reusable code with custom modules, which improves maintainability and decreases redundancy. For instance, a group developing a web application may design distinct modules to manage user authentication, database operations, and API integrations. This kind of functionality division makes the codebase easier to test and more modular. On the other hand, developers can arrange these modules into a logical structure that mirrors the application's general design by using custom packages. For collaborative projects, this hierarchical structure is especially helpful because it enables team members to work on multiple packages at once without interfering with one another's work.

Advanced features like relative imports and dynamic imports are supported by Python's modular design. Relative imports make it easier for developers to access related functionality by enabling them to reference modules inside the same package or directory. Conversely, dynamic imports allow modules to be imported during runtime in response to certain circumstances. These characteristics provide Python programming more adaptability, which facilitates the creation of effective and flexible programs. But in order to steer clear of dangers like dependence problems and cyclical imports, companies also need a firm grasp of the underlying ideas.

Modules and packages are essential to testing and debugging, two processes that are essential to the development process. Developers can test individual components separately before incorporating them into the overall system by separating functionality into discrete modules. Because problems can be linked to certain modules, this modular approach to testing makes it easier to find and fix defects. Python code is frequently tested using tools like unit test, pytest, and doctest, which integrate easily with modular designs. With the use of these tools, developers may create test cases for every module, guaranteeing that the code satisfies the necessary requirements and operates as intended.

Modules and packages excel in documentation as well. Developers can make it simpler for others to comprehend and utilize the code by breaking functionality down into distinct components and providing clear, short documentation for each module. With Python's built-in docstring capability, programmers may provide documentation about the functions, inputs, and outputs of classes and functions right in the code. Because team members can rapidly understand the operation of various modules without a lot of external documentation, this self-documenting method not only improves code readability but also makes collaboration easier.

Another benefit of using modules and packages is that they encourage code reuse, which is essential to effective programming. Reusability minimizes the requirement for redundant code by enabling developers to take advantage of pre-existing solutions for common issues. For example, with very minor changes, a module created for managing file operations in one project can be utilized again in another. This guarantees uniformity across many apps in addition to saving time. Furthermore, because reusable code has been applied to a variety of situations and circumstances, it is frequently more reliable and thoroughly tested.

Python code's modular design makes it easier to implement version control, a crucial technique in contemporary software development. Developers can monitor changes to individual components of code without impacting the entire source by grouping code into modules and packages. Teams can coordinate changes, settle disputes, and keep track of revisions with version control systems like Git. In collaborative settings, when several developers are working on the same project, this is especially helpful. Because Python code is modular, modifications made to one module won't unintentionally affect other areas of the application.

The adaptability of Python's modules and packages is demonstrated in a variety of fields and applications, demonstrating their usefulness in actual situations. Frameworks like Flask and Django, for example, are designed with modular principles in web development, enabling developers to import only the components required for a given project. This strategy guarantees that the apps will continue to be flexible and lightweight. Modular architecture also helps data scientists and analysts use tools like Pandas, Matplotlib, and Scikit-learn. These libraries' module-based structure streamlines workflows and increases computing performance by allowing users to access particular capabilities without needless overhead.

Modularity is much more important in the context of scientific inquiry and computers. Highly specialized modules for mathematical and scientific computations, ranging from linear algebra to signal processing, are available through Python libraries such as NumPy and SciPy. By using these tried-and-true modules to carry out intricate tasks, researchers can concentrate on their areas of expertise. Because scientists may share and reuse modules that are specific to their specialties, this modular architecture not only speeds up research but also promotes collaboration across disciplines.

Additionally, the modular structure makes it easier to integrate Python with other platforms and technologies.

For example, certain modules that encapsulate the underlying protocols and interactions are frequently necessary for Python's compatibility with databases, cloud services, and external APIs. The complexity of these integrations can be decreased by developers using modules like SQLAlchemy for database administration, boto3 for AWS services, and requests for web APIs. Python is still a popular option for creating scalable, cloud-based, and networked applications because of its versatility.

It is impossible to overestimate the educational advantages of Python's modularity. Modules provide novices with an approachable starting point for programming, enabling them to concentrate on particular subjects without being intimidated by the intricacy of a full-fledged application. In order to develop a thorough understanding of Python programming, educators might create lesson plans that are modular and gradually introduce key ideas. Conversely, more experienced students might focus on developing unique modules and packages and learning about best practices for software architecture and design. Python is the perfect language for teaching programming at all skill levels because of its versatility.

The concepts of modularity and packaging foster community involvement and open-source contributions. A sizable developer community supports the Python ecosystem by producing and maintaining third-party packages and contributing to open-source repositories like GitHub and PyPI. Because Python programming is modular, contributors can concentrate on particular modules or features without having to know the entire codebase, which facilitates collaboration. This decentralized strategy has produced a thriving and creative community that consistently pushes the limits of Python's capabilities.

Other areas where Python's modules and packages shine are automation and scripting. The tools required to automate file handling, system functions, and process management are provided by modules such as OS, Shutil, and Subprocess. Developers can decrease the possibility of human mistakes, increase efficiency, and automate repetitive operations by creating modular scripts. These scripts are quite useful in a variety of industries, from marketing and finance to IT and DevOps, because they are simple to distribute and modify.

Using modules and packages also improves security and dependability. Critical functionality can be isolated within specialized modules, allowing developers to carry out exhaustive testing and implement specific security measures. To reduce the possibility of vulnerabilities, for instance, encryption and authentication features can be contained within secure modules. Because individual modules may be patched or replaced without affecting the application as a whole, the modular structure also makes updates and maintenance easier.

As technology develops and the need for effective software solutions increases, modules and packages will play an increasingly important role in Python development. Python's modular environment is already being used by cutting-edge industries like blockchain, quantum computing, and artificial intelligence to address difficult problems. The modularity principles will continue to be at the heart of the creation of new libraries and frameworks, guaranteeing Python's continued status as a flexible and progressive programming language.

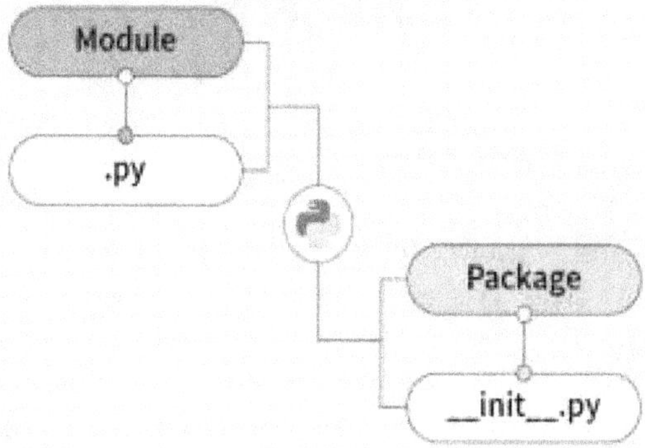

To sum up, modules and packages are essential components of Python programming that let programmers create reusable, scalable, and maintainable code. These constructs improve the organization, readability, and collaboration of code by breaking functionality down into discrete parts. A strong framework for managing intricate codebases is offered by the import system, namespaces, and package hierarchy. Python's capabilities are increased by third-party packages and tools like pip, which let programmers take advantage of the combined knowledge of the international Python community. Additionally, the modular design makes testing, debugging, and documenting easier, which guarantees the creation of software of the highest caliber. The ideas and procedures surrounding modules and packages will continue to be essential to Python's success as it develops further, enabling programmers to produce creative and effective applications.

CHAPTER IV

Advanced Python Programming

Decorators and Generators

Two of Python programming's most potent and adaptable capabilities are decorators and generators, which give programmers the means to create clear, effective, and readable code. Python's utility is greatly increased by these characteristics, which let programmers abstract repetitive activities, manage intricate control flows, and create dynamic behavior. Their usage highlights Python's advantages as a language that can be used by both novice and expert programmers due to its deep functionality and ease of use.

In Python, decorators are high-level concepts that allow you to extend or change the behavior of functions or methods without changing how they are actually implemented. Decorators are essentially functions that take another function as input, perform some extra operations, and then return the altered function. They are, therefore, a sophisticated way to handle issues like validation, logging, authentication, and memoization. Decorators wrap these duties rather than immediately embedding them into a function's body, resulting in code that is more organized and modular. A layered structure that improves code maintainability can be created by developers by stacking several decorators on top of a single function, each of which fulfills a different function. One of the fundamental principles of software engineering, "separation of concerns," is in line with this design principle.

Decorators are extremely useful for a wide range of applications because of their versatility. Decorators are essential for sending HTTP requests to the right view functions in web development frameworks like Flask and Django. Decorators enable developers to describe routes concisely while preserving the readability of the application, eliminating the need for repeating code to map URLs. Decorators simplify test case definitions in unit testing by applying setup or teardown actions automatically. In a similar vein, decorators can impose user authentication, guaranteeing that only those with permission can access confidential data. These illustrations demonstrate how decorators can be used practically to address issues in a variety of fields.

Decorators demonstrate Python's grammatical elegance in addition to their usefulness. The @ sign, which was first used as syntactic sugar, enables developers to use decorators in a clear and understandable manner. Even for people who are not familiar with the underlying decorator technology, this makes code easier to read and comprehend. Decorators enable developers to concentrate on more complicated programming tasks by abstracting away complex logic, which increases code quality and productivity.

In contrast, Python structures such as generators make it easier to create iterators. Generators produce numerous values over time, suspending their state between calls, in contrast to typical functions that only return one result. This eliminates the memory overhead of building and storing complete data structures in memory, enabling developers to work effectively with big datasets or continuous streams of data. The `yield` keyword is used to define generators, offering a sophisticated method of generating data dynamically.

When large-scale data processing or streaming is involved, the benefits of generators become clear. For example, traditional functions that load everything into memory would not be able to read a large text file line by line or generate an unending sequence of numbers. Generators, on the other hand, guarantee effective resource use by enabling developers to create and consume data incrementally. Because of this functionality, generators are essential to Python's ability to handle large data and real-time applications.

The capacity of generators to facilitate lazy evaluation—in which calculations are postponed until their outcomes are required—is another intriguing use case. The idea of maximizing performance by minimizing pointless computations is consistent with this principle. In scientific computing and machine learning, where handling big datasets and intricate mathematical models necessitates careful resource management, lazy evaluation is very helpful. Generators offer a simple method for building pipelines that process data incrementally, guaranteeing that tasks are carried out only when necessary.

Advanced patterns like coroutines, which enable two-way communication between the generator function and the caller, are also supported by generators. Developers can enable dynamic data manipulation and interactive processes by passing data back into the generator using the `send` method. Applications like simulation, real-time analytics, and event-driven programming will be significantly impacted by these capabilities. Python's asynchronous programming architecture is based on coroutines, which are built on top of generators and are essential for creating scalable, non-blocking systems.

The strength and versatility of Python are further demonstrated by the combination of decorators and generators. When combined, they enable developers to apply reusable design patterns, improve the functionality of pre-existing functions, and produce unique iterators. Decorators, for instance, can be used to encapsulate generator functions and add timing, logging, or exception handling to their functionality. This synergy bridges the gap between readability and performance by allowing developers to build code that is both expressive and efficient.

Although decorators and generators might be difficult for novices to master, Python's dedication to providing developers with cutting-edge tools is demonstrated by their inclusion in the standard library. Python's community resources and documentation offer thorough instructions, making these ideas understandable to a wide range of users. The adaptability of decorators and generators is further demonstrated with tutorials, examples, and open-source projects, encouraging developers to investigate their possibilities in novel and creative ways.

Teaching decorators and generators exposes students to fundamental programming ideas like closures, higher-order functions, and state management from an educational standpoint. These ideas are essential to comprehending contemporary programming paradigms and are not specific to Python. Gaining proficiency with decorators and generators gives developers abilities that they can use with a variety of languages and technologies.

Decorators and generators will probably play a bigger part in Python's ecosystem as it develops further. These capabilities are constantly being incorporated into new frameworks and libraries to improve their usability and functionality. For instance, the incorporation of decorators and generators into asynchronous programming models highlights their applicability in tackling modern issues like parallelism and concurrency. Developers can create applications that are scalable, resilient, and efficient by utilizing these tools.

The usage of decorators and generators in dynamic code creation and metaprogramming is another example of their adaptability. The ability of decorators to alter the behavior of classes, methods, or entire modules at runtime makes it possible to create software that is incredibly flexible and customized. On the other hand, generators make it easier to create dynamic data pipelines whose content and structure can change in response to real-time inputs. These sophisticated use cases demonstrate the breadth and complexity of Python's architecture, which strikes a compromise between ease of use and the capacity to handle challenging programming tasks.

Python's ability to solve both common and highly specialized jobs is demonstrated via decorators and generators. Their use extends beyond theoretical frameworks to real-world situations that call for effectiveness, adaptability, and clarity. Developers can access a higher degree of abstraction by thoroughly knowing these tools, which frees them from becoming mired in ineffective solutions or repetitive code patterns and enables them to concentrate on problem-solving.

Additionally, decorators are now essential for improving code readability and reusability in collaborative settings. Because they centralize the handling of cross-cutting issues and remove repetition, they clearly play a part in upholding the DRY (Don't Repeat Yourself) philosophy. In collaborative projects, where maintaining uniformity across codebases may otherwise become a daunting chore, this is very helpful. Decorators ensure uniformity and time efficiency by allowing teams to design a behavior once and apply it consistently across several functions or methods.

In contrast, generators are becoming more and more popular as data-driven applications require increasingly complex solutions for managing streams and repeating calculations. Generators are becoming more important than ever due to the rise of big data and the growing dependence on real-time analytics. The scalability of applications handling terabytes of data is supported by generators, which enable the development of data pipelines that process information incrementally. They lessen the requirement for high memory usage, which is essential for contemporary applications where performance and usability are directly impacted by efficiency.

Additionally, the use of decorators and generators has become more accessible due to their incorporation into frameworks and libraries. Because these functions are easily integrated into intuitive APIs, developers no longer need to fully understand the underlying mechanisms in order to utilize them. For example, generators in libraries like Pandas or NumPy streamline data transformation and computation workflows, while decorators in web frameworks like Django encapsulate complicated routing or middleware functionality. Developers of various skill levels can effectively utilize these functionalities because of their ease of adoption.

Powerful opportunities in asynchronous programming are also made possible by the combination of decorators and generators. The combination of decorators and generators guarantees smooth operation in asynchronous tasks, such as reading files, retrieving APIs, or managing databases, where processes take place simultaneously. While generators give tasks the structure they need to produce outcomes without preventing execution, decorators make managing asynchronous workflows easier. As demonstrated by contemporary web servers and microservices architectures, this synergy produces scalable systems that can manage thousands of connections at once.

These capabilities' compatibility with Python's explicitness and simple ethos is another significant feature. Although decorators and generators might appear sophisticated at first, their use and implementation adhere to Python's fundamental design concept, which is to help programmers produce legible and manageable code. This feature is what makes Python so strong and user-friendly for a broad spectrum of users, from novices to pros.

The ongoing development of Python's core tools, such as decorators and generators, is inextricably related to the language's future. These tools will adjust to new paradigms and difficulties as programming evolves. These Python features are probably going to be included in the basic workflows of emerging industries like blockchain technology, artificial intelligence, and machine learning. While generators might effectively handle the massive amounts of data produced by these technologies, decorators may expedite the development of machine learning pipelines or enforce security standards in blockchain systems.

Gaining proficiency with decorators and generators requires both technical and conceptual knowledge. These characteristics inspire developers to think creatively and create elegantly functional solutions. In the dynamic field of programming, where originality and imagination are just as crucial as technical know-how, this way of thinking is priceless. Developers push the limits of what Python can accomplish as they investigate the possibilities of decorators and generators, helping to expand the ecosystem as a whole.

To sum up, decorators and generators are not just Python features; they are paradigms that represent the language's philosophy of offering strong, adaptable, and user-friendly tools. They are essential to contemporary software development because of their capacity to streamline difficult tasks, improve performance, and promote good coding habits. By becoming proficient with these technologies, developers may fully utilize Python and prepare themselves to face obstacles in a quickly evolving technical environment. These characteristics will continue to play a crucial role in determining how Python programming develops in the future and how it affects the larger software development industry.

To sum up, decorators and generators are essential components of Python programming that exemplify the language's values of elegance, functionality, and simplicity. They give programmers strong tools to construct modular, effective, and maintainable code, tackling problems in fields including data analysis, web development, scientific computing, and asynchronous programming. Python is the go-to option for developers looking to construct creative and effective applications because of its diversity and synergy, which show off the depth of its capabilities. Decorators and generators will continue to be at the heart of Python's success as it develops and adapts to the demands of contemporary computing, encouraging programmers to push the limits of what is conceivable with code.

Working with APIs

Knowing how to use APIs in Python is an important skill for coders. It helps them create applications that can connect and work with other software systems. APIs, or Application Programming Interfaces, are tools that help different software programs communicate with each other. They allow these programs to share information and carry out tasks without needing to see each other's code. This feature is essential in today's digital world, supporting everything from social media and payment systems to weather apps and online shopping. Python is very popular for working with APIs because it has a lot of libraries and easy-to-understand syntax, which makes the process quick and straightforward.

APIs work as intermediaries, defining a set of rules and protocols for interaction. When using APIs in Python, writers usually send and receive data by making HTTP requests. This process often uses tools like `requests,` which makes it easier to send different types of HTTP requests like GET, POST, PUT, and DELETE. Python works well with JSON, which is a popular data format used in APIs. This makes it easier for Python to handle replies from APIs. You can easily read and work with JSON data in Python, helping developers gather useful information or take needed steps based on that data. Python's tools are easy to use, so even newbies can quickly learn how to work with APIs.

A popular use of APIs is to get info from outside sources. For example, a weather API can give you up-to-date information about the temperature, humidity, and rain for a specific place. In Python, developers can send a GET request to the API, including the needed parameters, and get the answer in JSON format. After receiving the data, it can be shown in an app, saved in a database, or analyzed further. This process saves time and removes the need to gather and enter data by hand, making apps work better and faster.

Authentication is very important when using APIs, especially when dealing with private information or services. Many APIs need developers to use credentials like API keys, tokens, or OAuth for identification. Python libraries like `requests-oauthlib` make it easy for developers to manage authentication and safely use APIs. By using secure login methods, developers can make sure their applications follow best practices and keep user data safe from unwanted access. This part of using APIs highlights the need to understand safety rules in software development.

Python can work with different kinds of APIs, like RESTful, SOAP, and GraphQL APIs. RESTful APIs are the most widely used. They do not keep track of previous interactions and use standard HTTP ways. Python's `requests` library is great for using RESTful APIs because it offers a simple and easy way to make requests and manage replies. SOAP APIs are not as popular, but they are still used in business applications and use XML for communication. Libraries like `zeep` help Python developers use SOAP APIs easily. You can use Python tools like `graphql-client` or `gql` to easily access GraphQL APIs, which let you query data more efficiently. These tools offer a consistent way to work with different API designs, highlighting how flexible Python is.

APIs allow developers to not only get data but also send data or take steps in other systems. For example, a social media API lets an app post updates, share pictures, or get user profiles. Python makes it simple to create and send requests with the right data, tags, and login details. Being able to connect with other systems like this creates many opportunities for automation, integration, and customizing. Developers can create apps that easily connect with other services, improving features and user experience.

Handling errors is also very important when using APIs. API contacts can fail for different reasons, such as network problems, wrong settings, or server issues. Python has strong error-handling tools, like try-except blocks, that help writers deal with problems smoothly. By using error-handling methods, developers can make sure their applications keep working well, even when problems arise. Logging and debugging tools help find and fix problems, making it easier to create dependable and easy-to-use apps.

Python has many advanced tools and packages for working with APIs. Flask and Django are two popular web tools that help writers build their own APIs. Flask is a simple and flexible framework that works well for small projects or prototypes. On the other hand, Django has many built-in features and can handle bigger applications better. Using these tools, developers can create APIs that allow outside users or systems to access their applications' features. This skill is especially useful for making microservices, which are small, separate parts that talk to each other through APIs.

Using APIs to automate repetitive jobs is a common practice, and Python is very good at it. For example, a developer might use an email API to send automatic messages, a payment gateway API to handle payments or a cloud storage API to control files. Python's ability to write scripts and its wide range of libraries make it simple to create programs that work with these APIs. This cuts down on manual work and boosts productivity. Using APIs for automation makes tasks smoother and helps keep things consistent and accurate, which is very important for business operations.

The increase in APIs has helped the development of products that use data. APIs from platforms like Google, Twitter, and OpenAI allow users to access a lot of data and use advanced features like understanding language and machine learning. Python can use libraries like Pandas and NumPy to handle and examine data from APIs, helping to find insights or make predictions. Using APIs and data science together has led to new developments in areas like healthcare and banking, where analyzing data in real time is very important.

APIs are very important in today's DevOps techniques. Jenkins, Kubernetes, and Docker have APIs that help developers automate the deployment, scaling, and monitoring of apps. Python works well with these tools, making it easy to include them in DevOps processes. This helps boost productivity and shorten the time it takes to bring products to market. Using APIs to automate infrastructure management helps businesses be more flexible and quickly adapt to new needs.

The collaborative nature of APIs has driven the development of open ecosystems where coders can build on each other's work. GitHub is an example of a platform that offers tools for managing projects and processes through APIs. Python developers can use these APIs to build tools that improve teamwork, like automatic reviewers for pull requests or scripts for release. This open method encourages new ideas and speeds up the creation of new technologies.

Testing and describing APIs are important for making sure they work well and are easy to use. Python libraries like `pytest` and tools like Postman help writers check if API endpoints work well, run efficiently, and are secure. Tools like Sphinx and Swagger make it easier to create detailed API docs, helping other developers use the API effectively. By focusing on testing and instructions, developers can create APIs that are of good quality and easy to use.

The increasing use of APIs in today's software development highlights the need to understand them well. Python is easy to use and has many helpful libraries, making it great for working with APIs. You can use it to get data, automate tasks, or create connections between different services. By learning about APIs, developers can build strong applications that use features from other systems, leading to new ideas and better user experiences. As APIs keep changing, Python's flexibility makes it a popular choice for coders in this important field of programming.

As more people want connected systems and services, APIs are becoming more important in programming and software creation. Knowing how to work with APIs is essential for developers who want to build strong and efficient applications. Python has a simple syntax and a wide range of libraries and frameworks, which helps developers quickly add APIs to their projects. This makes it one of the most flexible programming languages available.

Adding APIs to Python projects can greatly improve what the applications can do. Python developers can build powerful and interactive applications by using external data, tools, and services. This integration allows apps to connect with other services. This means they can get live info, send alerts, manage files, or handle transactions. There are many options available, and Python is easy to learn, making it perfect for quickly working with APIs.

Python offers tools that help with security, like managing OAuth, API keys, and tokens, so developers can create safe apps. Authentication is important when using APIs, and Python's libraries make it easy to set up safe ways to access other services. By using good security practices, developers can keep important data safe and make sure their applications work securely in different situations.

As technology improves, APIs will play a bigger role in software creation, especially as more people want cloud-based solutions and connections with other platforms. Python can work with various types of APIs like RESTful, SOAP, and GraphQL, making it easier for developers to create strong and easy-to-manage apps. By learning how to integrate APIs, Python developers can build creative applications that will adapt to the changing needs of users and groups.

In summary, APIs are important for today's software development, and Python is a great choice for coders to work with them. By learning how to use APIs, Python writers can access external services, combine data from various sources, and automate tasks that used to be done by hand. This creates many chances to build applications that are full of features, can grow easily, and are safe. As software development changes, knowing how to use APIs and Python will be important for workers who want to build effective solutions in a connected world.

Concurrency and Parallelism

The principles of concurrency and parallelism are extremely significant in contemporary computing, particularly in programming languages such as Python. These are fundamental strategies that help enhance the performance of programs by allowing tasks to be completed simultaneously rather than sequentially. This optimization helps applications run better. When it comes to situations in which numerous activities need to be performed simultaneously, such as analyzing huge datasets, handling multiple requests in a server, or executing difficult computations, these ideas are very significant. The goal of both concurrency and parallelism is to improve the efficiency of a program; however, they accomplish this goal in different ways. It is essential to have a clear grasp of the differences between the two in order to make good use of them.

Software is said to have concurrency when it is able to handle numerous tasks at the same time. However this does not necessarily mean that it can do so concurrently. Due to concurrency, separate components of a program are able to make progress without having to wait for each other to finish, which gives the impression that parallelism is being achieved. This is accomplished by managing numerous jobs in such a way that the software alternates between them. This enables the system to handle more work at the same time despite the fact that the individual activities may still be executed in sequential order. Concurrency is frequently utilized in order to enhance the responsiveness of a program. One example of this is in web servers, which are responsible for simultaneously processing several client requests.

On the other hand, parallelism is the process of carrying out many jobs at the same location at the same time. In a parallel system, a task is broken down into smaller subtasks that are then completed simultaneously. This is accomplished by using several processors or cores to break the task into smaller elements. Applications that demand a substantial amount of processing power, such as scientific simulations or jobs involving machine learning, are perfect candidates for this option. Because Python is a high-level language, it offers a number of different ways of implementing parallelism. This enables developers to make the most of multi-core processors, which in turn speeds up the execution of their programs.

Within the realm of Python programming, it is essential to make a distinction between concurrency and parallelism. Python was developed with the intention of handling concurrency and parallelism in a certain manner. One of the most important aspects that determines how concurrency and parallelism can be achieved in Python is the Global Interpreter Lock, sometimes known as GIL. The GIL is a technique that assures that it is only possible for a single thread to execute Python bytecode at any given moment, even on computers that have many cores. Because of this limitation, it may be difficult to make full use of several cores when executing Python code, particularly when performing operations that just require the CPU. Python, on the other hand, offers a wide variety of tools and methods that can be utilized to circumvent the GIL constraints and successfully implement concurrency and parallelism.

Using threads is one of the most frequent techniques to create concurrency in Python. Threads are used to implement concurrent processing. Using the `threading` module in Python, developers have the ability to generate several threads of execution within a single process. The fact that each thread operates independently, even if they share the same memory area, makes it simple for them to communicate with one another. The GIL, on the other hand, prevents threads in Python from running in parallel when they are assigned CPU-bound tasks. Threads are especially useful for I/O-bound tasks, which are processes in which the application spends a significant amount of time waiting for external resources. Examples of such tasks include handling network requests or reading and writing to disk. Therefore, in situations like these, while one thread is waiting for an input/output operation to finish, other threads can continue to execute, which ultimately results in an improvement in the application's overall performance.

Python provides a module called "multiprocessing" that enables developers to construct several processes, which is useful for jobs that require genuine parallelism. Processes, in contrast to threads, have their own memory space, which means that they do not directly share data with one another. Because of this, they are perfect for CPU-bound tasks, which are jobs in which the GIL is a bottleneck. Python is capable of achieving true parallelism, which enables the application to make full use of the capabilities of multi-core processors. This is accomplished by generating many processes, each of which runs on its own core. The `multiprocessing` module offers a range of features, including process pools and queues, which simplify the management of many processes and facilitate the coordination of communication between them.

One more method for achieving concurrency in Python is to employ asynchronous programming, which is enabled by the `asyncio` module. Asynchronous programming is very helpful for tasks that are I/O-bound, which are tasks in which a program spends a substantial amount of time waiting for events that occur outside of the program. To manage these tasks, asynchronous programming allows the program to run a single thread and halt execution while waiting for I/O operations to finish. This is an alternative to the traditional method of creating numerous threads to handle these tasks. At this point, the software is able to switch to another task, allowing it to make effective use of the resources it has available. In Python, the `asyncio` module offers a framework that facilitates the construction of asynchronous code. This framework employs constructs such as `async` and `await` to effectively handle tasks that are executed simultaneously.

Python is equipped with a number of third-party libraries and frameworks that can assist with concurrency and parallelism. These libraries are in addition to the built-in libraries that are already present. For instance, the `concurrent.futures` module offers a high-level interface that allows for the execution of function calls in an asynchronous manner. Classes such as `ThreadPoolExecutor` and `ProcessPoolExecutor` are provided by it, which enable developers to handle threads and processes in a manner that is both straightforward and easy to understand. The implementation of concurrency and parallelism in Python applications is simplified as a result of these classes, which abstract away a significant portion of the complexity needed in managing instances of processes and threads.

Not only does the difficulty of concurrency and parallelism involve the management of many processes or tasks, but it also involves the management of the complications that occur as a result of multiple activities interacting with shared resources. The occurrence of race conditions, which take place when many threads or processes attempt to access or modify shared data at the same time, is a common problem that arises in concurrent programming practices. This can result in behavior that is difficult to predict, as well as issues that are particularly challenging to reproduce and fix. Locks, semaphores, and events are some of the synchronization techniques that Python offers in order to reduce the likelihood of race conditions occurring. It is possible for developers to regulate access to shared resources through the use of these technologies. This ensures that only a single thread or process can make changes to the resource at any given moment.

Concurrency and parallelism both provide new obstacles despite the fact that they offer significant performance improvements. Because of the non-deterministic nature of execution, debugging concurrent and parallel applications can be a challenging endeavor. It is easier to recreate and correct defects in a single-threaded program because the order of execution is predictable. However, in a concurrent or parallel program, the order in which tasks are completed can change, which makes it more difficult to diagnose and fix bugs. Furthermore, the management of communication and synchronization between processes can be a challenging endeavor, particularly in applications that are distributed on a wide scale. Despite the fact that Python's tools, such as the `multiprocessing` and `async` modules, offer techniques to address these difficulties, developers must nevertheless be aware of the various hazards that may arise when dealing with concurrency and parallelism.

In spite of these obstacles, concurrency and parallelism are powerful techniques that have the potential to greatly increase the performance and efficiency of Python applications. It is possible for developers to take advantage of the power of multi-core processors, handle numerous I/O activities simultaneously, and construct programs that are both responsive and scalable if they make use of the appropriate tools and approaches. This ecosystem is available regardless of whether the developer is working with threads, processes, or asynchronous programming. In the years to come, the ability to work with concurrency and parallelism will become an increasingly vital talent for Python developers. This is because multi-core computers and distributed systems are expected to continue their rapid expansion.

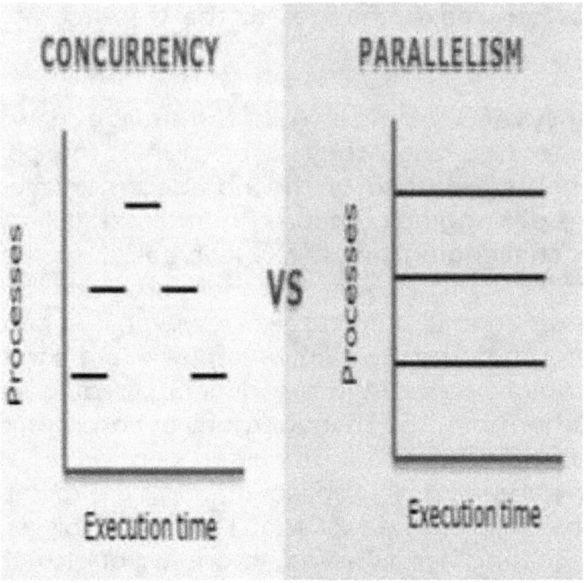

To summarize, concurrency and parallelism are fundamental ideas in Python programming that enable developers to create programs that are not only responsive but also scalable and efficient. Developers are able to optimize their code to handle several jobs simultaneously, take advantage of multi-core processors, and increase the overall performance of their applications if they have a thorough understanding of the distinctions between these two strategies and have mastered the tools that are available in Python. Despite the fact that concurrency and parallelism each come with their own unique set of difficulties, Python offers a comprehensive collection of tools and packages that can assist developers in overcoming these hurdles and maximizing the potential of concurrent and parallel programming. The mastery of concurrency and parallelism will be an essential ability for Python developers as the demand for applications that are both faster and more efficient continues to grow. This will enable them to construct high-performance systems that are able to satisfy the requirements of modern customers and businesses.

CHAPTER V

Practical Projects

Project 1: Simple Budget Tracker

Applying several core Python principles, including variables, control structures, functions, and data structures, is necessary to create a project like a basic budget tracker. By monitoring income and costs and offering a straightforward method for classifying and calculating spending, a budget tracker aims to assist users in managing their money. This section will give a thorough rundown of the project, including everything from the application's conception to the specific procedures for creating and improving it with Python.

The initial step in creating a budget tracker application is to comprehend the program's goals and requirements. A budget tracker must enable users to enter financial information, including income and expenses, classify these entries, and generate summaries that provide insight into the user's financial situation. Features like adding new transactions, showing the list of transactions, figuring out the overall balance, and producing reports on spending categories might all be included in the tracker.

How to organize the data is one of the most important factors. A straightforward method for storing transaction data in Python would be to use dictionaries or lists. A dictionary with keys like "description," "amount," and "category" might be used to store each transaction. It would be simpler to comprehend what each value signifies if dictionaries were used to provide descriptive descriptions for each entry. A flexible and user-friendly method of managing transaction data is offered by dictionaries, which make it simple to add, remove, or alter individual entries as needed.

Following the establishment of the fundamental framework, the functionality for adding new transactions must be implemented. Usually, this would entail developing a function that lets the user input information like the transaction amount, category, and description. The command line or, if preferred, a basic graphical user interface (GUI) would be used by the user to enter this data. To help the user keep track of their spending, a prompt may inquire about the type of transaction (revenue or expense), the amount, and an optional category. The user would be able to analyze their spending and learn more about where their money is going with the aid of categories like "Food," "Rent," "Utilities," and "Entertainment."

Users should be able to check their past transactions as well as create new ones using the budget tracker. This might be accomplished by writing a function that outputs a list of transactions, arranged according to their type, along with pertinent details like the transaction's date and amount. Printing each transaction on a different line while iterating through the list is a straightforward way to accomplish this. The output can be clearly formatted so that the user's financial history is easy to read and comprehend.

The capacity to compute the current balance is a crucial component of a budget tracker. All income entries are added together, and all spending entries are subtracted to accomplish this. By iterating through the list of transactions, the computer may compute the total income and total expenses, then subtract the latter from the former to display the current balance. Python makes it simple to sum numerical numbers. Calculating totals for each category could also be helpful in letting the user know how much money they are spending on various aspects of their lives. This gives the user information on areas where they might be able to reduce their spending and increase their savings.

Creating reports or summaries is another feature of the budget tracker. A helpful report may provide a monthly breakdown of revenue vs expenses or the amount spent in each area over a certain time period. These reports can be made by combining transaction data, classifying the transactions by date or category using Python's data structures, and then summarizing the data through calculations. Users can make better financial decisions with the help of this information.

After the fundamental features are established, user input validation and error management should be taken into account. Any program that accepts user input must take into consideration the potential for inaccurate or unexpected inputs. For instance, users may inadvertently type characters rather than numbers when entering sums, or they may submit a negative value for income. This can be resolved with Python by utilizing error-handling features like try-except blocks, which detect faults and prevent the program from crashing. The program is made more reliable and user-friendly by verifying input and making sure that only legitimate data is accepted.

Additional functionality, including the ability to save and load data to and from a file, could be added to the application to further improve the budget tracker. This would enable the user to keep track of their balance and transaction history across sessions. Reading and writing data from external files is made simple by Python's file management features. For instance, the data may be saved to a file whenever a new transaction is added, and the software may load the saved data to continue where it left off upon restarting. By adding persistence, users may be sure that they won't lose their transaction data when they close or reopen the program.

A more advanced user interface would also improve the budget tracker. Although the command line interface (CLI) or terminal can be used to create the basic version of the tracker, Python has a number of modules that developers can utilize to create graphical user interfaces (GUIs). By allowing the construction of windows, buttons, and input fields, libraries like Tkinter or PyQt make it possible for users to interact with the application in a more natural and user-friendly manner. A GUI might have buttons for adding or removing transactions, dropdown menus for choosing categories, and a display area for summaries and reports.

Another crucial factor to take into account for a project like a budget tracker is security. Even while a basic budget tracker might not need sophisticated security features, it is still crucial to make sure that private financial data is managed safely. This can be accomplished by encrypting files, storing data in a safe format, or asking users for their passwords if the application needs them. For a more sophisticated version, it could be worthwhile to investigate the possibility of using bank APIs or online payment providers to enter transactions into the budget tracker automatically.

An essential part of the development process is testing the budget tracker application. Developers can make sure the software functions as intended and that faults are identified prior to the application's release by testing its many features, including adding transactions, calculating balances, and producing reports. Python has a number of unit testing tools, including the unit test module, which may be used to automate the testing procedure and confirm that every application component is operating as intended.

Following the development and testing of the basic budget tracker, it's critical to think about how to make the application even better. Advanced capabilities such as the ability to generate graphs and visualizations of spending patterns, for instance, can assist users in better understanding their financial circumstances. With the use of Python libraries like Matplotlib and Seaborn, programmers may construct a variety of charts, including pie charts and bar graphs, to show spending trends or categories over time. In addition to giving consumers clear, useful insights, these visualizations can enhance the budget tracker's user experience.

Budgeting goals are another way to improve the budget tracker. The application would allow users to set spending targets for certain categories and monitor their progress toward those targets. For instance, if the user has established a monthly grocery budget of $300 or less, the computer may notify them when they are getting close to that amount. Users may be more inclined to follow their spending plans and make better financial decisions as a result of this feature.

Documenting the code and giving future users and developers clear instructions are crucial as the project moves forward. The maintainability of the project and the ability of others to comprehend how the application functions are both enhanced by well-written documentation. This includes generating a README file that describes how to use the application, its features, and how to install or run it, as well as adding comments to the code that clarify important functions and logic.

There are innumerable ways to enhance and broaden the basic budget tracker, considering the size of the project. Integrating the application with third-party financial services, like bank accounts or payment systems, is one possible improvement. Users would be able to see their transactions instantly loaded into the budget tracker, doing away with the need for human entry if the tracker were connected to real-time data from credit cards or banks. Financial institution APIs or third-party services might be used to provide this feature, which would enable the tracker to safely retrieve transaction data and instantly update the budget.

Enhancing the user experience is another crucial issue that can be resolved. Although a command-line interface can be used, a web application or mobile app would greatly improve the tracker's accessibility by offering a more elegant and user-friendly interface. Developers can produce user interfaces that are both aesthetically pleasing and intuitive by using frameworks like Kivy for mobile development or web development tools like Flask or Django. The tracker would be more accessible and practical while on the go if users could, for example, create their accounts, monitor their spending, and view their budgets straight from their desktops or mobile devices.

Adding tools like warnings and notifications would give consumers real-time guidance as the project becomes more complex. For instance, users might get reminders to record their spending or notifications when they are about to go over their allocated budget in a certain category. Email alerts or push notifications could do this. Users may be able to set financial objectives using the tracker, like saving for a trip, and receive alerts when they are meeting or exceeding those objectives.

Additionally, the application would enable users to maintain thorough records for future reference or tax purposes by enabling them to export their budget data in formats like CSV or PDF. Users could create printable reports that give an overview of their financial activity over a specific time period or examine their data in spreadsheet applications like Google Sheets or Excel.

With this new capability, the tracker would be more useful than just a tool for keeping track of daily spending.

Incorporating sophisticated statistical research would also provide users with a better understanding of their financial habits. To help customers anticipate future expenses, the tracker may, for instance, use predictive algorithms to forecast future spending trends based on historical data. The tracker can offer actionable insights that enable users to make better financial decisions by utilizing Python libraries such as NumPy, Pandas, and Scikit-learn to help with data analysis and machine learning. In addition to improving the tracker's functionality, these sophisticated features would provide each user with a more customized experience.

Testing and debugging are still essential processes in guaranteeing the stability and dependability of the budget tracker, just as in any software project. It is crucial to keep an eye out for bugs, performance problems, and edge cases that can occur during user interaction with the application. To ensure that the application functions properly in a variety of scenarios and maintains its performance as new features are added, automated testing can be used. While integration tests can be used to confirm that the various components of the program function as a cohesive whole, unit tests can be created to make sure each component operates as intended.

Another important component of the development process is user feedback. Developers can find problems or areas where the application needs improvement by gathering input from test users or early adopters. User feedback can direct the creation of upcoming updates, whether they focus on problem fixes, new feature additions, or interface simplification. Establishing a feedback loop makes sure that the tracker changes to suit user requirements, which eventually results in a more popular and successful application.

To sum up, building a basic Python budget tracker is a terrific approach to hone your programming abilities and provide a practical financial management tool. This project covers a wide range of crucial Python programming principles, from establishing the fundamental framework for managing transactions to including more complex features like file processing, reporting, and graphical user interfaces. Developers can tackle each component methodically and progressively create a fully functional budget tracker by segmenting the project into smaller parts. Users will learn more about their spending patterns as they engage with the app, which may aid them in making wiser financial choices. The budget tracker project can be improved and expanded in countless ways as Python develops further, giving developers plenty of chances to advance their knowledge and produce even more potent applications down the road.

Project 2: API-based Weather App

Learning how to handle JSON data, communicate with external services, and create useful applications is all made possible by utilizing Python programming to create an API-based weather app. Such a project's objective is to obtain current meteorological data from a public API and display it in an approachable way. Working with APIs, processing data, and arranging that data for display are all skills you would acquire during this process. In addition to being a fantastic method to hone your Python abilities, this kind of project is also a terrific way to learn how apps communicate with outside data sources.

Selecting the appropriate API service is the first stage in creating a weather app that uses APIs. OpenWeatherMap, WeatherAPI, and other weather APIs are among the numerous that are available online, both for free and for a fee. The majority of these services give developers access to a variety of weather-related information, including forecasts, historical weather data, and current weather conditions. In order to authenticate requests and guarantee that the service is being used correctly, developers typically need to register for an API key in order to use these APIs. Developers can start creating the queries to retrieve the weather data once they have the API key.

Sending an HTTP request to the API endpoint is the next step. This is usually accomplished in Python with the `requests` package, which enables developers to submit HTTP requests in an easy-to-understand way. The required information, including the location for which the meteorological data is being sought, is included in the request. The requested weather data is subsequently returned by the API, often as a JSON object. Numerous meteorological parameters, including temperature, humidity, wind speed, and the kind of weather (cloudy, rainy, or sunny), are contained in this JSON object. The next step after retrieving the data is to parse it into a format that can be used.

An essential component of using APIs is parsing the JSON response. Because it is lightweight, readable, and compatible with the majority of programming languages, including Python, the JSON format is frequently used in API communication. Python's `json` module offers tools for processing and parsing JSON data. The weather information can be shown to the user in the weather app project by extracting the parsed JSON data. Developers may decide to display the data in a straightforward text style or in a more structured manner with several components, such as the current temperature, humidity level, and wind speed presented separately, depending on how complicated the app is.

The next task after parsing the data is to arrange and display it to the user in a way that is clear and easy to comprehend. Developers can show the data in a simple graphical user interface (GUI) application or on the command line for a rudimentary weather program. In order to make the weather data more aesthetically pleasing and accessible, creators of more sophisticated weather apps could decide to produce a web or mobile application. Simple GUI applications can be made with Python's `Tkinter` module, while web-based weather apps can be made with web development frameworks like Flask or Django.

The weather app can be enhanced with new features to improve the user experience. Requesting the weather for several cities or places is one helpful feature. The software can provide weather information for a variety of locales by letting the user enter the name of a city or their GPS coordinates. This feature increases the app's versatility and adds engagement. Giving consumers a weather forecast for the next several days is another improvement that might be made. This can be done by obtaining data from the relevant API endpoint that offers forecast information. By adding new features to the software, the project gains sophistication and provides the user with greater value.

Error handling is another crucial aspect to take into account. Robust error handling is crucial since working with APIs frequently entails addressing network problems, erroneous requests, or inaccurate data. The application should check for problems such as invalid API keys, inaccurate location inputs, or server outages while submitting an API request. The software can recover gracefully from problems and give the user insightful feedback if errors are handled properly. For instance, the app can notify the user that the weather data is unavailable and ask them to try again later if the API request is unsuccessful because of a network problem.

Developers should concentrate on improving the app's performance in addition to its useful aspects. Depending on the data being sought and the speed of the server, API requests may occasionally be delayed. Developers may use caching, which keeps the output of API requests locally for a predetermined amount of time, to lessen this. The application's overall efficiency is enhanced, and the burden on the API server is lessened by caching the weather data to prevent the app from requesting the same information repeatedly. Caching may greatly speed up response times, which is especially helpful for weather apps because the data may not change often.

Developers can concentrate on enhancing the app's usability and style once the essential functionality is in place and it is operating correctly. Users' interactions with the app are significantly influenced by how the weather data is presented. While a cluttered interface may lead to confusion, a simple and clean design can help consumers access the information they need more easily. With distinct labels for every item of meteorological data and an intuitive navigation method, developers should strive for an aesthetically pleasing and intuitive design. While mobile apps can be created using tools like Kivy or React Native, web-based weather apps can be created with front-end technologies like HTML, CSS, and JavaScript to create an eye-catching interface.

The software can also be made more user-friendly by giving users useful features like the option to switch between Celsius and Fahrenheit units or the display of a weather indicator that corresponds to the current weather state. To improve the app's visual attractiveness and give it a more interactive feel, it may also show a backdrop image that changes according to the weather (sunny, rainy, snowy, etc.). Users may find the app more entertaining and engaging with these little but significant enhancements.

Two essential phases in the development process are testing and debugging. The user experience may be impacted by even a little mistake in the data parsing or weather information display. To make sure that all features function as intended and that the app handles failures appropriately, it is crucial to test the app extensively. To ensure that each of the app's separate parts—such as the display function, data parsing function, and API request function—is operating as intended, unit tests can be created. Before the software is made available to consumers, developers can find and address flaws by running these tests.

Developers may keep adding new features and enhancing the user experience as the app develops. For instance, customers who wish to keep an eye on long-term patterns might find it useful to have a tool that lets them track the weather over time. As an alternative, the app might be able to automatically determine the user's position and provide the local weather by integrating with a location-based service, like GPS. Developers can improve the app's functionality, usefulness, and usability by iterating on it frequently.

The development of the app also heavily relies on testing and troubleshooting. Maintaining the integrity of the application depends on making sure that edge cases—like erroneous city names or unsuccessful API requests—are handled appropriately. Obtaining weather data is only one aspect of the problem; another is presenting it in a trustworthy, consistent, and error-free manner. Developers may resolve any problems and make sure the program works as intended under all conditions by creating unit tests and carrying out exhaustive manual testing.

User comments must also be taken into consideration. Listening to customer feedback and grievances after the app is released is crucial since it can reveal critical information about what features users find most helpful and what needs to be improved. Developers may make sure the software stays useful, relevant, and functional by iterating it frequently in response to user feedback.

Developers can keep improving the weather app by adding new features and methods as new tools and technologies become available. The app might become even more inventive by, for instance, including machine learning techniques to forecast future weather trends or interacting with additional IoT devices to offer more individualized weather data. The software is kept interesting, engaging, and able to adapt to the changing needs of its users thanks to this continuous process of development and improvement.

To sum up, building a Python weather app with an API offers a practical learning experience that encompasses a variety of programming ideas, such as interacting with external APIs, managing JSON data, designing user interfaces, and putting error handling into practice. By including features like weather predictions, multi-city support, and speed improvements, developers may make an app that is both user-friendly and adaptable to the demands of users. While creating a practical application that other people may use, this project provides the chance to practice critical Python skills. In addition to expanding knowledge of Python programming, the project offers insightful information about how to develop a fully functional, API-driven application.

Project 3: Basic Web Scraper

One of the most interesting and practical projects for Python beginners is building a simple web scraper. In order to complete this project, data must be taken from websites and formatted such that it may be processed or analyzed further. Python is a great option for creating web scrapers because of its ease of use and robust tools. Choosing a website to scrape data from is the first thing to think about when beginning a web scraping project. Selecting a website with a clear and consistent structure is crucial. Web scraping works best on websites with structured data, such as job advertisements, product listings, or news stories.

Getting the required tools is the next step after choosing the website. BeautifulSoup and requests are the two main Python libraries used for web scraping. A Python package called BeautifulSoup offers straightforward ways to navigate, explore, and alter the parse tree—a web page's HTML structure. Data extraction from HTML texts needs it. As an alternative, the Requests library is used to send HTTP requests to the website and obtain its HTML content. When these two libraries are used together, the webpage can be requested and parsed to retrieve valuable information.

There are multiple steps involved in creating a simple web scraper. The required libraries must be imported first. The requests library is then used to retrieve the webpage when the libraries have been imported. Sending a GET request to the website's URL does this. The page's HTML content is returned after a successful retrieval. However, the HTML content is not user-friendly and requires parsing in order to be searchable and readable. Here's where BeautifulSoup can help. Once the HTML material has been passed into BeautifulSoup, it parses it and generates a parse tree that makes it simple to edit and traverse across the HTML structure.

Identifying the webpage parts that require scraping is the next stage in the construction of the web scraper. HTML tags like <div>, <span>, <a>, <p>, and <h1> are commonly used on websites to organize their content. Targeting particular items on the page is possible with these tags' various properties, such as class names or

IDs. The web scraper's task is to extract the needed material by navigating through the parsed HTML structure. Several BeautifulSoup functions, including search(), find_all(), and select(), can be used to accomplish this. With the help of these functions, you can look for HTML components using various parameters, such as tag name, class, or ID.

The scraper can extract the needed data after locating the pertinent pieces. If the website has a list of product names, for instance, the scraper can take the text out of those names and save it for later use. To concentrate primarily on the pertinent content, this data extraction method may entail removing extraneous components like navigation bars and ads. Cleaning up and formatting the data into a more usable manner is frequently the following step after data extraction. This could entail dealing with any special characters that could be in the data, eliminating excess whitespace, or changing the text to lowercase.

Depending on the intended usage, the web scraper's retrieved data can be saved in a variety of formats. CSV, Excel, and JSON are examples of common formats. These formats make it simple to store data for analysis and subsequent processing. After being saved, the data can be entered into programs like Pandas, a well-known Python data analysis toolkit. This allows for the analysis, cleaning, and manipulation of the scraped data to produce reports or obtain new insights. Numerous opportunities for work automation, information gathering, and research are made possible by the capacity to pull data from the web and store it in an organized fashion.

Although creating a basic online scraper is a fairly simple process, real-world website scraping presents several difficulties. Because they are dynamic, websites have the ability to evolve throughout time. This implies that if the HTML structure of the website is altered, a web scraper that functions well today could not function well tomorrow. Developers must be aware of these developments and ready to modify their scrapers as necessary. Furthermore, certain websites might include safeguards against web scraping. Rate restriction, CAPTCHAs, and restricting IP addresses that send too many requests are a few examples of this. Understanding web scraping best practices is necessary to overcome these challenges, which may entail putting strategies like IP address rotation, increasing delays between requests, or CAPTCHA solving into practice.

The ethical and legal ramifications of scraping data from websites are another factor to take into account when developing a web scraper. Reading and comprehending a website's terms of service is crucial because some websites have strict guidelines on the usage of their data or forbid scraping. It is essential to make sure that web scraping is carried out responsibly and ethically without infringing on website owners' rights or overloading their servers with requests. An API may be offered by certain websites to give users more regulated and organized access to their data. In these situations, leveraging the API rather than simply scraping the page might be a better course of action.

There are numerous chances to improve and broaden the capabilities of the basic web scraper once it is operational. Increasing the scraper's durability is one method to make it better. To make sure the scraper can deal with problems like network outages, timeouts, or missing items, this can entail implementing error handling. To make the scraper easier to use, developers could also wish to create a user interface. Users can choose the data they want to extract, input the URL of the website they want to scrape, and choose how they want the data to be saved using a straightforward graphical user interface (GUI).

The demand for efficiency and scalability increases with the complexity of web scraping applications. Adding support for asynchronous programming or multithreading is one technique to increase a scraper's scalability. When scraping huge webpages, this speeds up the process by enabling the scraper to make numerous requests at once. Furthermore, sophisticated web scrapers would have to handle pagination, which entails obtaining information from several website pages. It can be challenging to handle pagination properly since it frequently calls for tracking the current page number and sending queries to several URLs.

Additionally, scraping JavaScript-generated dynamic content can be more difficult than crawling static HTML. JavaScript is used by many contemporary websites to load data dynamically, which means that the material is not in the HTML when the page first loads. Developers might need to employ extra tools, like Selenium, to manage a web browser and mimic user activities in order to load dynamic material before scraping it.

A simple web scraper can be used for a number of real-world purposes, such as tracking news stories, monitoring job postings, and collecting data for market research. Web scraping can be used in the business sector to track prices, monitor online sentiment, and provide competitive data. Web scraping can be used in research to acquire big datasets for analysis, observe trends over time, or collect data for investigations.

Building a web scraper can also provide an experience that can be applied to more complex tasks. You can proceed to more complicated projects like developing web crawlers that can examine numerous pages and websites, incorporating machine learning models to evaluate the data that has been scraped, or using web scraping as a tool for data mining and big data analysis once you have mastered the fundamentals of the technique.

The demand for improved error handling increases with the complexity of web scraping initiatives. A crucial component of creating a dependable tool is making sure the scraper can recover from unforeseen problems and handle mistakes graciously. Try-except blocks, debugging logging, and alerting users to unsuccessful scraping efforts may all be part of this. Additionally, developers may keep an eye on the scraper's activity and determine when and where it finds errors by putting in place more advanced logging methods.

Additionally, a lot of online scraping jobs entail duties beyond straightforward data gathering. For instance, developers could wish to use graphs or charts to display the data that was scraped. In this situation, data visualizations can be made straight from the scraped data using libraries like Matplotlib and Seaborn. As an alternative, the scraped data may be preprocessed and examined for trends or patterns before being fed into machine learning models.

Developers may also run into scalability issues as the web scraping project's scope expands. Performance problems may occur, especially when scraping huge pages or when using scrapers on several websites at once. Developers can use concurrency strategies like threading or asynchronous programming to lessen these problems. Threading speeds up the scraping process by enabling the scraper to perform numerous tasks at once. When a scraper must manage numerous slow network queries without interfering with other operations, asynchronous programming can be quite helpful.

For scraping jobs that are really demanding, a distributed solution could be required. This entails distributing the workload among several computers or servers in order to manage extensive data extraction projects. The distribution of jobs can be managed using technologies like Apache Kafka or distributed task queues like Celery, guaranteeing that the scraper operates effectively even when dealing with massive volumes of data.

With increasing sophistication, web scraping can be used for a wide range of purposes in various sectors. For instance, businesses can use competitor website scraping in e-commerce to monitor product availability and pricing trends. Web scraping can be used in journalism to track social media sentiment or collect information for investigative reporting. Web scraping can be used by marketers to monitor brand mentions on the internet or by researchers to gather big datasets for analysis. Automating the process of gathering data from websites creates a wealth of opportunities for creativity and understanding in a variety of fields.

The field of web scraping has changed over time. With the development of new methods and equipment, scrapers can now perform tasks that are more complicated. Many websites have also taken steps to identify and stop scraping, like restricting IP addresses that send too many queries or using CAPTCHAs. In order to overcome these obstacles, developers working on web scraping projects need to be aware of them and continuously modify their approaches.

The use of machine learning and artificial intelligence technologies in web scraping projects has emerged as a major topic of interest as these technologies continue to develop. Web scrapers' accuracy and efficiency can be increased by developers through the use of machine learning techniques. The scraping process can be improved by using machine learning, for example, to automatically identify pertinent information on a page. Additionally, the scraper can comprehend context and collect more pertinent information by using natural language processing (NLP) techniques to extract meaning from textual input.

Developing a "crawler," a program that can automatically browse a website and recursively scrape data from several pages or domains, is another more sophisticated method of web scraping. When working with websites that have several levels of pagination or navigation, web crawlers are especially helpful. Developing an effective web crawler requires addressing issues, including handling big datasets, maintaining state between queries, and making sure the crawler doesn't become trapped in endless loops.

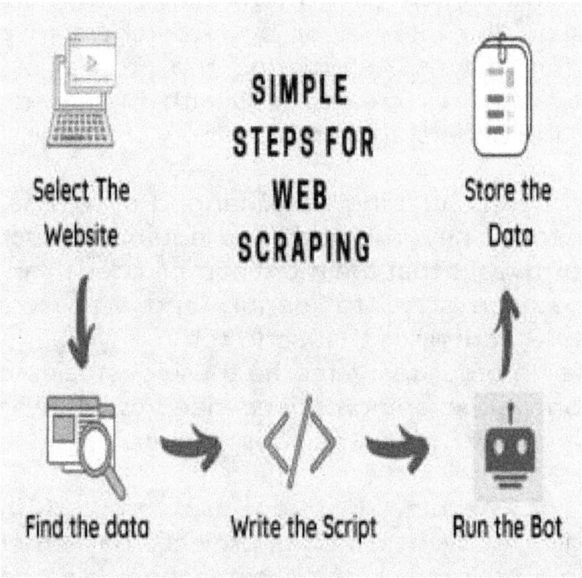

To sum up, a simple web scraper is a great project for anyone learning Python since it teaches a number of crucial skills like automation, data retrieval, and data parsing. Even though the project isn't very complicated, it provides a framework for more intricate and scalable web scraping programs. Through this project, developers learn how to handle mistakes, deal with dynamic content, and observe legal bounds while also gaining invaluable experience working with web technologies. In the end, developing a web scraper gives you a firm grasp on how to collect information from the internet and convert it into a format that can be used for additional processing or analysis.

CHAPTER VI

Mastering Python Tools and Libraries

NumPy for Numerical Computing

NumPy, short for Numerical Python, is one of the most important libraries in the Python ecosystem, particularly for scientific computing. It is an effective tool for working with high-level mathematical functions, matrices, and arrays. Developed for data-intensive applications, NumPy offers an efficient method for managing sizable datasets and carrying out intricate numerical calculations. A multi-dimensional container for components of the same type, the array object and array, is the foundation of NumPy. Since it makes it possible to manipulate big datasets quickly and effectively—a crucial component of many scientific, financial, and machine learning projects—the array is the foundation of the majority of scientific computing jobs in Python.

Python's built-in list data structures are significantly slower than NumPy's array capability. One of the primary causes of NumPy's widespread use is its speed. Because of its vectorized operations, which allow operations on whole arrays to be carried out in parallel, explicit loops are typically not necessary. This feature makes code simpler, easier to comprehend, and easier to maintain, in addition to increasing performance. The core component of NumPy is the array object, which offers an adaptable and memory-efficient method of storing and working with data. It can perform tasks like broadcasting, slicing, element-wise arithmetic, and advanced indexing.

NumPy provides a variety of methods to carry out intricate mathematical calculations in addition to its fundamental array manipulation features. Fourier transformations, random number creation, linear algebra, and other complex mathematical procedures are all incorporated into it. Additionally, NumPy offers a range of array manipulation, resizing, and aggregation tools—all essential for effectively managing data in engineering and scientific research projects.

Essential operations for working with vectors and matrices are provided by NumPy's linear algebra routines. For instance, it facilitates the solution of linear equation systems, matrix multiplication, eigenvalue decomposition, and dot products. These performance-optimized functions are extremely quick and efficient, which makes NumPy perfect for computationally demanding applications like data science, physics simulations, and machine learning. Furthermore, NumPy comes with tools for handling random numbers, which are crucial in domains like machine learning and statistics. Among the many random number generation features offered by the random module is the ability to take samples from different probability distributions.

NumPy's capability for broadcasting, which enables actions between arrays of various forms, is another important feature. NumPy can carry out element-wise operations even when the operands have different widths thanks to broadcasting. This feature can be used to operate on arrays of different sizes and dimensions and eliminates the need for explicit loops. For example, if the shapes are compatible with broadcasting rules, broadcasting can be used to add a scalar to an entire array or to perform element-wise actions between arrays of various forms.

Users can extract subarrays and manipulate arrays in a variety of ways thanks to NumPy's support for slicing and advanced indexing. A useful feature that makes it possible to retrieve particular parts of an array without changing the original data is slicing. In addition to supporting multi-dimensional slicing, it may be used to extract rows, columns, or certain items. By enabling more intricate indexing, such as choosing non-contiguous elements or filtering array elements using boolean conditions, advanced indexing expands on existing functionality.

NumPy's ability to integrate with other Python libraries is another crucial feature. NumPy is the foundation for several other libraries in the Python scientific computing ecosystem, including SciPy, Pandas, and sci-kit-learn, which depend on it for effective data manipulation. For instance, the underlying data structure for the Series and DataFrame objects in the well-known data analysis tool Pandas is NumPy arrays. Working efficiently with these higher-level libraries requires familiarity with NumPy, as these libraries heavily rely on NumPy's array-oriented operations to maximize speed.

Additionally, NumPy has several benefits in terms of memory management. NumPy arrays are more memory efficient than Python lists because they are stored in continuous chunks of memory. This storage format enhances performance when carrying out computationally demanding operations and lowers the overhead needed to manage massive datasets. Additionally, NumPy provides tools for managing array memory layout, including the ability to select the row-major or column-major order of memory components. In some situations, this control may be helpful for optimizing memory access patterns.

NumPy comes with a number of tools for reading and writing data to and from different file formats in addition to its basic functions. It makes it simple to save and load data for additional analysis by supporting the reading and writing of data in binary and text forms. Through the use of third-party libraries like Pandas and h5py, NumPy also facilitates compatibility with other data formats, such as CSV, Excel, and HDF5.

NumPy's versatility makes it suitable for a broad range of applications. NumPy is frequently used in data science to handle and analyze big datasets, carry out statistical research, and put machine learning methods into practice. Because of its performance benefits, which enable effective data processing and manipulation, it is perfect for these activities. For example, NumPy is used in machine learning for tasks like feature engineering, data preprocessing, and the application of algorithms like neural networks, k-means clustering, and linear regression.

NumPy is an essential tool for numerical simulations in domains such as physics, engineering, and finance due to its performance and memory efficiency. It can be applied to financial data analysis, physical system modeling, and differential equation solving. For instance, NumPy is frequently utilized in signal processing tasks in engineering, where the frequency components of signals are analyzed using fast Fourier transforms (FFT). NumPy is used in finance for options and derivatives pricing, portfolio optimization, and risk analysis.

NumPy is frequently used in conjunction with other libraries, such as SciPy and Matplotlib, in scientific computing to carry out intricate simulations, resolve optimization issues, and produce visualizations. Building upon NumPy, SciPy offers a suite of extra scientific computing tools, including signal processing functions, integration procedures, and optimization techniques. In contrast, Matplotlib is used to create interactive, animated, and static data visualizations. These modules work together to create a robust Python toolbox for data analysis and scientific computing.

The impact of NumPy is not limited to the Python community. NumPy's array-based approach to data manipulation has served as an inspiration for numerous other programming languages and numerical computing environments, including R and MATLAB. Due to its widespread use, NumPy has become the de facto standard for numerical computing in Python, and data scientists and engineers frequently learn it as their first Python library. It has a sizable and engaged user base, and the NumPy community is still actively involved in its advancement.

Enabling Python to effectively manage huge datasets is one of NumPy's most important contributions to the Python ecosystem. Python is renowned for its flexibility and ease of use, but its built-in data structures—like lists—are not well-suited to managing big information. By offering an effective, adaptable array object that can easily manage big datasets, NumPy overcomes this restriction. One of the main reasons NumPy is so widely used in domains like data science, machine learning, and scientific computing is its capacity to handle massive datasets.

Additionally, NumPy's design facilitates integration with other tools and libraries. It is an obvious choice for usage in other libraries and frameworks because of its array data structure's simplicity and adaptability. NumPy arrays are frequently used as the base data format for more specialized tools and libraries since they are simple to pass between functions and libraries. For instance, NumPy arrays are frequently used in machine learning to store the weights and biases in neural networks as well as to represent the input features and target variables for models.

With frequent updates and enhancements to the core library and related tools, the NumPy ecosystem keeps developing. With constant additions of new features and improvements, NumPy is becoming an even more potent Python tool for numerical computation. NumPy is still one of the most popular Python libraries, and its development was driven by the demands of the scientific computing community.

From a research standpoint, NumPy is vital to scientific simulations, where numerical accuracy and high performance are critical. For computationally demanding operations, researchers may rely on NumPy's optimized numerical routines, whether they are doing simulations in physics, biology, chemistry, or engineering. For simulating intricate systems and resolving mathematical models that are impossible to manage with more conventional programming techniques, NumPy has emerged as the preferred tool.

The effectiveness of NumPy is also crucial in the financial industry, where quick and precise numerical computations are needed to price derivatives, simulate financial markets, and assess risk. NumPy is used by quantitative analysts to create financial models and carry out tactics like risk management, portfolio optimization, and option pricing. Financial firms can perform real-time quantitative research and high-frequency trading thanks to their effective handling of massive datasets.

NumPy's built-in functions are not the only ones that support linear algebra and more complex mathematical procedures. Because of its array format, NumPy can also communicate with specialized libraries like LAPACK (Linear Algebra PACKage), which offers functions for eigenvalue decomposition and linear system solving. The usefulness of NumPy for intricate numerical calculations is further enhanced by this degree of integration.

Furthermore, NumPy's robust third-party library ecosystem keeps growing, extending its capabilities beyond its fundamental capabilities. NumPy arrays are used as the foundational data structures by libraries such as SymPy (for symbolic mathematics) and PyTorch (for deep learning), demonstrating how NumPy's design philosophy has grown to be an essential component of the larger Python data science and machine learning ecosystem.

The importance of NumPy as a dependable and effective tool for numerical analysis only increases with the growing demand for data-driven decision-making across industries. NumPy continues to be the preferred Python library for scientific computing, regardless of whether one is working with large datasets, intricate mathematical models, or state-of-the-art machine learning algorithms. Because of its speed, memory efficiency, and user-friendliness, it is a vital tool for researchers and professionals in a wide range of fields.

To sum up, NumPy is a crucial Python module for numerical computation. It offers strong and effective tools for handling big datasets, carrying out intricate mathematical operations, and resolving issues in science and engineering. NumPy is a vital tool that can help you work more productively and efficiently, whether you are in data science, machine learning, scientific computing, or any other field that involves numerical processing. NumPy is still an essential component of the Python scientific computing ecosystem and has become the basis for many sophisticated Python programs due to its extensive functionality, outstanding performance, and smooth integration with other Python libraries.

Pandas for Data Manipulation

Pandas is an open-source library in Python that provides data structures and functions needed to manipulate structured data. Tasks including data analysis, data cleaning, and data visualization are often carried out with its assistance. Pandas is a data structure and data analysis tool created specifically for the Python programming language. Its primary purpose is to provide high-performance, user-friendly data structures. Due to the fact that it is one of the most widely used libraries for data manipulation, it has developed into an essential instrument within the information science ecosystem. In this section, we will investigate the fundamental functionalities of pandas, including their fundamental data structures and the ways in which they may be utilized to alter and analyze data.

The capability of pandas to manage data in a variety of formats, including CSV files, Excel spreadsheets, SQL databases, and JSON files, is one of the key reasons for the popularity of this programming language. Data scientists and analysts are able to input, process, and export data with ease thanks to its flexibility in reading and writing a variety of data types. The Series and the DataFrame are the two primary data structures that are utilized in Pandas. A Series is a labeled array that is one-dimensional and can carry a variety of data kinds. On the other hand, a DataFrame is a labeled data structure that is two-dimensional and has columns that could potentially be labels of different types.

For the purpose of data manipulation, Pandas offers powerful tools. It enables users to do operations such as filtering, sorting, and aggregating data, which makes it simpler to evaluate and extract insights that are helpful. Moreover, it offers the capability of merging, connecting, and altering datasets, which makes it an excellent tool for managing databases that are both extensive and complicated. Pandas are an indispensable tool for doing tasks such as data wrangling, cleansing, and transformation because of their skills with these features.

The process of data analysis typically includes a number of jobs, one of the most time-consuming of which is data cleaning. Through the provision of a wide range of methods that are able to identify and deal with missing values, duplicate entries, and incorrect data, Pandas makes this process more straightforward. As an illustration, pandas give users the ability to discover duplicate entries in a dataset, delete rows or columns that contain missing values, and fill in missing data with values that have been given or defined. Pandas are an invaluable resource for data scientists because of their capacity to swiftly clean and prepare data for examination.

Pandas are able to do complex indexing and slicing operations, which is another important aspect of this programming language. The process of gaining access to a particular component or subset of data included in a larger dataset is referred to as indexing. Pandas give users the ability to obtain and alter data in a variety of ways, including by allowing them to index and slice data based on labels or locations, respectively. Due to the fact that it can work with row labels as well as column labels, pandas are very effective when working with structured data that contains meaningful labels.

It is possible to perform many levels of indexing on rows and columns using the hierarchical indexing feature that is supported by pandas in addition to the standard indexing feature. In situations when a dataset may contain more than one level of categorization, this is very helpful because it allows for the possibility of working with multi-dimensional data. The ability to group data based on numerous criteria is made possible by hierarchical indexing, which also makes it simpler for users to carry out operations and calculations that are group-based.

Additionally, Pandas offers useful tools for time series analysis, which is an essential component of data manipulation in a wide variety of domains, including economics and finance, among others. It includes the capability for resampling, shifting, and rolling windows, as well as built-in support for processing time-based data by default. When working with data that is subject to fluctuation over time, such as stock prices or sensor readings, this is of utmost importance. When using

Pandas, analysts are able to effortlessly modify and analyze time-based data without the need for external libraries because of the time series functionalities that are available.

Pandas' capacity to carry out operations based on groups is among the most powerful features of this programming language. Using the group by function in pandas, users are able to group data based on one or more columns and then proceed to execute actions like aggregation, transformation, or filtering on each group of data. When working with big datasets that need to be segmented into smaller subsets that are easier to manage, this is a very helpful tool to have. In the field of statistical analysis, group-by operations are frequently utilized in situations when it is necessary to aggregate data based on particular categories.

In addition, Pandas has a wide range of operations that can be used to combine and consolidate datasets. Users are able to take various datasets and merge them into a single dataset through the use of these operations. This can be accomplished by matching rows based on similar columns or by adding rows from distinct datasets. When working with data from numerous sources that need to be merged for analysis, this is an extremely crucial consideration to keep in mind. Pandas provides users with a variety of joins to choose from, including inner joins, outer joins, left joins, and right joins, which allows them to combine datasets in a manner that aligns with their preferences.

It is not restricted to simple procedures when it comes to the capacity to alter and transform data capabilities. Data pivoting and unpivoting are two examples of the more sophisticated activities that may be performed with Pandas. Reshaping data is referred to as pivoting, and it involves transforming the values of a single column into many columns. Unpivoting, on the other hand, is the opposite of pivoting. In situations where users are working with datasets that are in wide or long formats, these transformations are helpful because they enable users to reorganize data in order to fulfill their analysis requirements.

A further benefit of using pandas is that it provides assistance when working with categorical data. A data set is said to be categorical if it can take on a limited number of unique values. Some examples of categorical data are product categories, gender, and geographies. This allows pandas to drastically reduce the amount of memory that is used and enhance efficiency when working with huge datasets. This is accomplished by transforming columns into categorical data types. When it comes to machine learning and statistical analysis, where categorical variables need to be handled in an efficient manner, this capability is quite helpful.

Within the realm of data visualization, pandas offer integration with other libraries, such as Matplotlib and Seaborn, to facilitate the creation of representations that are both insightful and informative. These features can be extended by users by utilizing specialized libraries to construct more complicated plots, such as histograms, scatter plots, and line graphs. Although pandas itself has basic charting capabilities, users can enhance these capabilities by using these libraries. Researchers are able to improve their understanding of the links between factors and their ability to successfully communicate their findings with the assistance of these representations.

The capability of pandas to efficiently manage huge datasets is just another one of its significant strengths. NumPy, a basic scientific computing library for Python, which offers efficient array operations, serves as the foundation upon which it is being constructed. This makes it possible for pandas to conduct data manipulation operations in a short amount of time, even when dealing with enormous datasets that might not fit into memory. Additionally, pandas offer options for working with data in chunks, which enables users to analyze enormous datasets piece by piece without encountering memory limits. This is made possible by working with data in pieces.

Pandas are not without their difficulties, despite the fact that they have many advantages. Its performance with really large datasets, which demand more memory than is typically accessible on a machine, is one of the potential aspects that could be considered a restriction. In these circumstances, users would be required to investigate additional tools, such as Dask or Vaex, which offer parallelized data processing for datasets that are larger than what can be stored in memory. There is also a steep learning curve connected with the wide functionality of pandas, which is another problem. It is possible for newcomers to feel overwhelmed when trying to comprehend the complete variety of options that are accessible despite the fact that Pandas offers a multitude of capabilities. Pandas, on the other hand, transforms into a highly effective and adaptable tool for data manipulation once users become familiar with its fundamental concepts and syntax.

Pandas is supported by a thriving community of users and contributors, which guarantees that the library will continue to develop and advance. Pandas receive regular updates and enhancements, which include the enhancement of existing features, the addition of new ones, and the correction of bugs. A further benefit of the robust community support is that users are able to readily locate documentation, tutorials, and examples that will assist them in learning how to make efficient use of pandas.

Streamlining the process of preparing data for machine learning models has been significantly facilitated by the development of Pandas. The process of preprocessing data is frequently one of the procedures that takes the biggest amount of time in the field of machine learning. Whether it's dealing with missing values, encoding categorical variables, normalizing numerical data, or dividing data into training and testing sets, pandas offer powerful capabilities that make it possible to execute these tasks in an effective manner. Pandas are an ideal companion for those who work in the field of machine learning because of how easily they can transform and structure data. As a result, they are able to concentrate on the process of model construction and evaluation without having to spend an excessive amount of time cleaning and arranging the data.

In addition, the capability of pandas to manage time series data is extremely useful for machine learning applications in a variety of domains, including finance, energy forecasting, and predictive maintenance. The process of modeling and evaluating data that is ordered in time, such as stock prices, weather patterns, or sensor measurements, is referred to as time series analysis. Users are able to execute operations such as resampling, time shifting, and windowing directly on time series data thanks to the specialized data structures that are provided by Pandas. One example of such a structure is the DatetimeIndex. When it comes to developing effective predictive models that rely on previous data to make predictions about future events, these features are absolutely necessary.

Besides its use in machine learning, pandas also play a key part in exploratory data analysis (EDA), which is a crucial first step in any data analysis project. This is because EDA is the first step in the process of analyzing data. An essential part of EDA is the process of summarizing and displaying the most important aspects of a dataset, which frequently involves the utilization of statistical graphics and charts. Pandas shine in this area because it offers a comprehensive collection of methods for rapid investigation. These methods include functions for generating descriptive statistics, displaying distributions, and determining relationships between variables. A better understanding of the underlying structure of the data, the identification of potential problems, and the determination of which variables are most relevant for subsequent analysis are all facilitated by this practice.

Due to the fact that it is integrated with other libraries, such as Matplotlib and Seaborn, Pandas has become an even more effective tool for exploratory data analysis. Data analysts are able to obtain deeper insights into the data and discover patterns that might otherwise go unnoticed if they combine the data manipulation skills of pandas with the graphical power of these libraries. By charting the distribution of a variable, for instance, an analyst is able to rapidly detect outliers or skewed distributions, which may suggest problems with the quality of the data or regions that need additional examination.

Moreover, the capability of pandas to manage categorical data has significant consequences for a wide variety of sorts of analysis techniques. Pandas provides the capability to efficiently manage and process categorical data through its categorical data type, which significantly reduces memory usage and speeds up computations. Categorical data is common in many datasets, where variables represent categories or groups, such as "gender," "region," or "product type." There are many datasets that contain categorical data. When dealing with huge datasets, when performance and memory management are of the utmost importance, this capability becomes very critical. Pandas enable the optimization of memory storage and the acceleration of operations such as sorting, grouping, and aggregating by transforming certain columns into categorical kinds.

Pandas excel in a number of areas, one of which is the management of data that is missing. Missing values are a typical problem in datasets that are based on real-world data, and it is essential to adequately manage them in order to conduct appropriate analysis. When it comes to dealing with missing data, Pandas offers a number of different solutions, such as filling missing values with a predefined value, forward or backward filling, or removing rows or columns that include missing data. The availability of these options provides analysts with the opportunity to select the strategy that is most suitable for their particular circumstances. Pandas ensure that analysts are able to continue their work without being slowed down by problems with the quality of the data they are working with by giving an easy solution to processing missing data.

One of the most typical challenges that arise while manipulating data is dealing with duplicated data, which is in addition to dealing with missing data. Errors that occur during the process of data gathering or the integration of disparate datasets might lead to the creation of duplicate entries. Pandas offers sophisticated capabilities that facilitate the identification and elimination of duplicates, thereby guaranteeing that analysts deal with data that is both clean and distinctive. Pandas is a very useful tool for data analysis for a number of reasons, one of which is that it can readily identify and deal with duplicates.

The ability to work with data that is organized into multiple levels is made possible by the fact that Pandas supports hierarchical indexing, which is one of its more advanced capabilities. This comes in especially handy when working with datasets that have multiple layers of categorization, such as sales data that is classified by both region and product category or financial data that is grouped by both company and time period. Hierarchical indexing allows analysts to combine data at several levels and conduct more complex operations on each group. This allows for greater flexibility and efficiency. Through this, one is able to gain more profound insights into the data, as well as conduct analysis that is more flexible and granular.

Pandas possess a number of significant features, one of which is the capability to carry out sophisticated data readability procedures. In order to conform to the specifications of a particular analysis or to conform to the structure of other datasets, it is frequently necessary to reshape the data involved. Several functions for pivoting and unpivoting data are provided by Pandas. These functions enable analysts to transform data from wide to long formats and vice versa. This is especially helpful when working with time series data or when preparing data for machine learning models, both of which include situations in which the format of the data may need to be modified in order to ensure compliance with particular statistical procedures.

One more essential characteristic that distinguishes Pandas from other data manipulation tools is its ability to provide scalable results. Although it is true that pandas might not be the greatest solution for managing big datasets that surpass the memory capacity of the system, it does offer choices for working with datasets that are larger than the memory capacity of the system. Using pandas, for example, users are able to process big datasets piece by piece since the programming language supports reading and writing data in chunks. When working with datasets that are too huge to fit into memory all at once, this chunking functionality is vital because it enables users to interact with the data in a manner that is both more efficient and less taxing on memory.

Pandas may also be coupled with other libraries and tools, such as Dask, which offers parallel processing capabilities for large datasets. This is another advantage of using pandas. Through the process of breaking down huge datasets into smaller, more manageable chunks and dividing the computation across numerous cores or even machines, Dask gives users the ability to conduct operations on datasets that are greater than the amount of memory available. Because of this, pandas is a flexible tool that can handle larger datasets even in contexts with limited resources. It can scale to manage additional data.

Pandas are equipped with a number of advantages, yet they are not without their drawbacks. When it comes to dealing with unstructured data, such as photographs, text, or audio, Pandas is not as efficient as it is when dealing with structured data. This is one of the limitations of the program. In situations like this, it is possible that other libraries, such as TensorFlow or PyTorch for machine learning, or libraries like OpenCV for image processing, would be better suitable. Pandas, on the other hand, continues to be the library of choice for efficiently managing structured data, particularly tabular data, and it is utilized extensively in data manipulation activities across a wide range of domains.

Therefore, when it comes to manipulating data in Python, pandas is an invaluable tool. As a result of its capacity to manage structured data, carry out sophisticated operations, and operate with a broad variety of data types, it has become an indispensable library for data scientists, analysts, and engineers. Pandas provides the tools that are necessary to efficiently manipulate and analyze data in Python. These tools include activities such as cleaning and transforming data, as well as performing complex analyses and visualizations. Because of its versatility and performance, it is one of the most extensively used libraries for data manipulation within the Python ecosystem. This is despite the fact that it has certain potential drawbacks. Pandas offers the functionality and flexibility necessary for efficient data analysis and manipulation, regardless of whether its users are working with tiny datasets or massive datasets that contain complicated information.

Matplotlib for Data Visualization

One of the most popular Python libraries for making static, interactive, and animated visualizations is called Matplotlib. The need to comprehend and interpret data has increased dramatically as it grows more complicated and prevalent in a variety of industries, including data science, machine learning, finance, and healthcare. Finding patterns, trends, and outliers in datasets is made easier for analysts and decision-makers with the aid of data visualization, and Matplotlib is a key tool for accomplishing this goal. It offers a flexible framework for creating a variety of plots, charts, and graphs that let users graphically depict data in a simple way to comprehend and analyze.

It is impossible to overestimate Matplotlib's importance in the data research environment. It makes it possible to quickly and easily create excellent visual representations of data. Matplotlib allows users to alter their plots to fit their needs, from the simplest line plots to intricate, multidimensional data representations. The library is frequently used with other libraries like Pandas, NumPy, and Seaborn to further streamline the data manipulation and visualization process. Although there are several other Python charting libraries, Matplotlib has maintained its position as the industry standard because of its extensive feature set, adaptability, and simplicity in integrating with other programs and libraries.

Matplotlib's ease of use and accessibility are two of its main selling points. The fundamental purpose of Matplotlib is to enable users to create visualizations with a comparatively minimal amount of code. Numerous plot kinds are supported by it, such as pie charts, line charts, bar charts, scatter plots, histograms, and many more. Users can easily create these charts and start evaluating their data by utilizing a limited number of methods. However, flexibility is not sacrificed for this simplicity. With the wide customization that Matplotlib provides, users can modify plot elements like colors, labels, titles, legends, and axes to suit their requirements.

The `plot` module, which offers a MATLAB-like interface for constructing visualizations, is the cornerstone of Matplotlib. This module enables users to create and modify graphs with commands recognizable to users who have worked with MATLAB or other comparable applications. By offering a straightforward and user-friendly vocabulary for plot generation, the `pyplot` module abstracts away a large portion of the complexity involved in constructing visualizations. Users can construct plots with personalized properties like markers, axis limitations, color, and line style by only invoking a few functions. Because of its simplicity of use, Matplotlib has become a vital tool for data scientists and analysts who need to efficiently and rapidly visualize their data.

In addition to standard plot types, Matplotlib facilitates more sophisticated visualization methods that let users understand their data more thoroughly. For instance, users can examine how one variable changes about another using contour plots and heatmaps, which are useful for showing correlations in huge datasets. Similar to this, box plots, violin plots, and stacked bar charts are crucial for comparing data categories and showing distributions. With these sophisticated methods, users can display complicated data in an understandable manner, making Matplotlib a vital tool for exploratory data research.

The ability of Matplotlib to manage several subplots inside a single figure is another important feature. Because it enables users to create many plots in a grid arrangement, this is very helpful for comparing disparate data sets side by side. More flexibility and control over the data display is possible with the ability to separately modify each subplot. When working with huge datasets, generating subplots is particularly helpful because different subsets of the data require different kinds of visualizations. Analysts can quickly examine trends, patterns, and relationships across their data by grouping several plots into figures.

Matplotlib offers a wide range of customization possibilities. Controlling how plot elements like lines, markers, and text look is one of the most crucial tools for personalizing visualizations. Users can change these elements' attributes, including line width, marker size, color, and style, using Matplotlib. To draw attention to particular data points or areas of interest, users can additionally annotate their plots. Annotations are very helpful for highlighting important plot points or giving the visualization more context. Additionally, Matplotlib makes it possible to personalize titles, legends, tick marks, and axis labels, guaranteeing that the plot is aesthetically beautiful and educational.

Additionally, Matplotlib supports many file formats for visualizations, making it simple for users to export their plots for use in publications, presentations, or reports. Depending on the intended output, it may export vector and raster pictures and supports popular file formats like PNG, JPEG, PDF, and SVG. Whether working in a digital presentation, print publication, or web environment, users may effortlessly incorporate Matplotlib-generated plots into their workflow because of the adaptability of the file formats.

Matplotlib's integration with other libraries expands its capabilities beyond its core features. For example, Matplotlib makes it simple to visualize data contained in

DataFrame objects when combined with Pandas. With Pandas' integrated charting features, which use Matplotlib, users may quickly create charts from their DataFrame. Thanks to this close connection, users may work fluidly between data processing and visualization activities, which speeds up the analysis and visualization process. Higher-level abstractions for statistical data visualization are also provided by libraries like Seaborn, which expands upon Matplotlib and offers even more potent capabilities for displaying intricate correlations in data.

Model evaluation is one of the most significant applications of Matplotlib in data science and machine learning. Understanding how well a machine learning model works requires visualization, and Matplotlib offers the resources required to create evaluation graphs, including precision-recall curves, ROC curves, and confusion matrices. Practitioners can evaluate their models' accuracy, precision, recall, and other performance indicators using these visualizations. Plotting these indicators makes it simple for practitioners to evaluate the effectiveness of various models and choose the best fit for their particular assignment. Additionally, models' learning curves may be seen during training using Matplotlib, which aids in spotting any problems like overfitting or underfitting.

Matplotlib is a vital tool in contemporary data analysis because of its capacity to produce interactive charts. Apart from static visualizations, Matplotlib facilitates the development of interactive charts that let users pan, zoom, and hover over data points to see more details. When working with enormous datasets, interactive graphs are particularly helpful since they let users explore the data more dynamically and interestingly. Matplotlib provides a basic level of interactivity that is enough for many use cases, even though its interactive features are not as sophisticated as those of certain other libraries, such as Plotly.

Matplotlib's popularity in the data science community has grown even more since it was integrated with Jupyter Notebooks. Users can integrate text, code, and visuals in a single document using the interactive environment that Jupyter Notebooks offers. Matplotlib in Jupyter Notebooks is a perfect tool for exploratory data analysis because it allows users to view their data while working. Plots can be shown inline within a Jupyter Notebook, allowing users to view the outcomes of their visualizations immediately without ever leaving the notebook environment. Matplotlib is essential to this approach, a common procedure in data science and machine learning.

Matplotlib has many drawbacks despite its great advantages. Compared to other visualization libraries like Seaborn or Plotly, which offer higher-level abstractions and more sophisticated capabilities right out of the box, this one can occasionally be clumsy despite being a strong tool for producing static representations. For instance, Seaborn, based on Matplotlib, offers a more straightforward interface for producing visually appealing statistical charts with little code. Plotly is a well-liked option for web-based apps since it provides a more user-friendly interface for producing dynamic visuals. Matplotlib is still the preferred tool for Python data visualization because of its unrivaled versatility and power.

Matplotlib's comparatively high learning curve for novices is another drawback. Even if the library has a lot of functions, it may take some time to become proficient with them all. Many of its more sophisticated capabilities, such as object-oriented programming and the structure of Matplotlib figures and axes, call for a better comprehension of the underlying ideas. Nevertheless, users can fully utilize the library's features to produce intricate and personalized visualizations if they are acquainted.

Because of its versatility, Matplotlib is frequently the library of choice for customers who need total control over their plots and visualizations. Professionals in industries like research and publishing, where accurate visualization formatting is essential, may find this feature of Matplotlib very helpful. Controlling every element of a plot, from font sizes to axis scale, guarantees that the finished product satisfies the highest requirements for quality and clarity. Higher-level libraries like Seaborn or Plotly, on the other hand, might abstract away part of this control to offer a more efficient experience, which might be better in situations that aren't as demanding.

The success of Matplotlib can be attributed in large part to its emphasis on a reliable and thoroughly described API. The library's developers have been working to keep the API stable and user-friendly over the years. Because of the API's consistency, users can switch between Matplotlib versions with ease and avoid learning a whole new set of tools or functions. Given the volume of users that depend on Matplotlib for their everyday work, this stability is essential to preserving the library's long-term usability. The comprehensive examples and tutorials in the documentation are also crucial in assisting users in comprehending how to use Matplotlib to address their data visualization issues.

Matplotlib's compatibility with other Python data analysis and manipulation packages is one area in which it excels. For instance, Pandas and Matplotlib work together effortlessly, enabling users to plot data straight from Pandas DataFrame objects. Effective processes for data analysis depend on the close relationship between data manipulation and visualization. Matplotlib offers a simple method for visualizing data, whereas Pandas facilitates the loading, cleaning, and manipulation of data. Because these two libraries are integrated, users may focus more on studying and interpreting the results rather than worrying about how to get their data ready for display.

The broad support from the open-source community is another factor contributing to Matplotlib's ongoing appeal in the data science field. Since Matplotlib is an open-source library, it gains from the additions and enhancements of programmers worldwide. As a result, the library has been able to change and grow to meet the requirements of the larger community. The open-source community's contributions have resulted in the creation of practical add-ons that increase the library's capability, as well as bug corrections and feature improvements. Matplotlib's ongoing development and support guarantee that it will continue to be a useful and potent tool for data visualization as the discipline of data science develops.

Matplotlib is a strong data visualization package, although it has considerable competition. Other libraries, such as Seaborn, Plotly, and Bokeh, offer other methods for visualizing data or higher-level functionality built on top of Matplotlib. For instance, Seaborn, which is based on Matplotlib, offers a more straightforward and user-friendly interface for making statistical plots that are visually pleasing. In contrast, Plotly and Bokeh concentrate on offering interactive visualizations with more sophisticated capabilities. Even while these libraries have certain benefits, particularly in terms of usability and interactivity, Matplotlib's strength and adaptability guarantee that it will always be an essential component of the data visualization ecosystem.

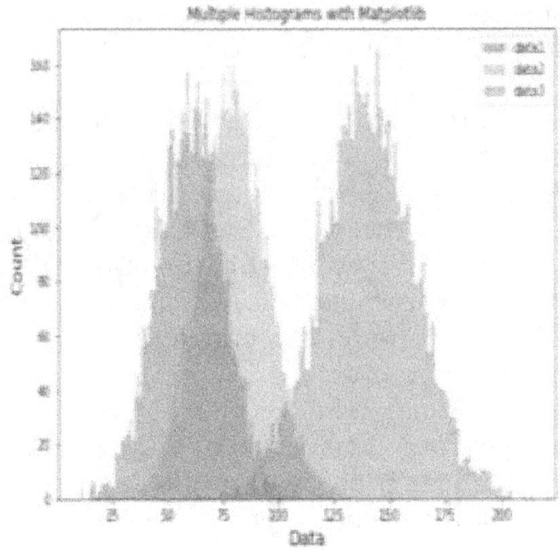

To sum up, Matplotlib is a crucial Python package for anyone dealing with data. It offers a wide range of visualization tools that let users show data in an aesthetically beautiful and educational manner. Matplotlib provides the adaptability and capability required to manage a variety of data visualization jobs, from simple plots to intricate representations. It is a flexible tool for both novice and expert users because of its support for interaction, integration with other Python libraries, and exporting capabilities for visualizations in several file formats. Matplotlib is still the preferred toolkit for producing excellent Python graphics despite its challenging learning curve and certain drawbacks. Its ongoing development and use guarantee that it will continue to be a vital component of the Python data science environment for many years to come.

CONCLUSION

Thank you for finishing "Mastering Python: From Basics to Expert-Level Programming: Learn Python Step-by-Step with Practical Projects"! You have studied Python fundamentals, intermediate programming methods, and more complex ideas like concurrency, object-oriented programming, and working with APIs. You have developed useful projects along the road that demonstrate Python's adaptability and usefulness in resolving real-world issues.

This book was created to give you a solid foundation in Python and the tools you need to take on challenging programming assignments. Along with learning Python's technical features, you've also learned how to solve problems, write effective code, and create applications that have an impact. You could put these ideas into practice through the practical tasks, which helped you learn more effectively.

But your adventure with Python doesn't stop here. Learning, trying, and honing your skills are all part of the ongoing programming process. With the skills and information acquired from this book, you're prepared to tackle more challenging tasks, delve into Python's vast library, or even focus on fields like machine learning, web development, or data science.

Keep in mind that practice makes perfect. Continue pushing yourself, maintain your curiosity, and don't be afraid to go over ideas again when necessary. Equipped with this understanding, you are now prepared to develop, invent, and leave your mark on the programming industry.

Thank you for buying and reading/ listening to our book. If you found this book useful/ helpful please take a few minutes and leave a review on the platform where you purchased our book. Your feedback matters greatly to us.

www.ingramcontent.com/pod-product-compliance
Lightning Source LLC
La Vergne TN
LVHW022059200926
848481LV00003B/993

* 9 7 9 8 3 4 9 2 6 9 9 8 1 *